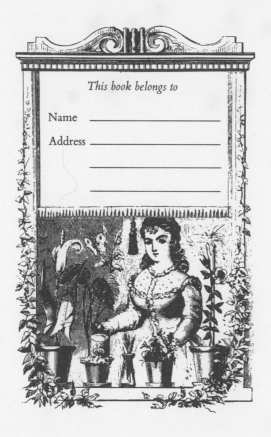

This book belongs to

Name _____

Address _____

_____

_____

SUPERWOMAN YEARBOOK

a home note book

SHIRLEY CONRAN

*Including
the Superwoman Diary for 1977
and Patric Walker's
Guide to Your Future in the Stars*

SIDGWICK & JACKSON

LONDON

With thanks to
Pauline Horrigan
Mileva Ross, Rosemary Lewis
Elizabeth Pomeroy, Donna McDonald, Nikki Knewstub
Prue Lightfoot, Jennifer Noll, Margaret Willes
Max Wright, Bill Procter, Malcolm Smythe

who put in so much careful work

and to British Gas
for their help and advice

Published in Great Britain in 1976
by Sidgwick & Jackson Limited

Copyright © Shirley Conran 1976

Your Future in the Stars
© Patric Walker 1976

ISBN 0 283 98334 5

Designed by Mike Ricketts

Printed in Great Britain by
The Garden City Press Limited
Letchworth, Hertfordshire, SG6 1 JS
for Sidgwick & Jackson Limited
1 Tavistock Chambers, Bloomsbury Way
London WC1A 2SG

Cover illustration
Drawing of a hydrangea,
probably for a flower book,
by A. Power, c.1800.
(Victoria & Albert Museum; photograph by John Webb)

Endpaper illustration
Engraving of the residence of John Nesbitt Esq.
(Metropolitan Toronto Library Board, Canada)

Acknowledgements
The quotation on p. 218 is taken from *Riders in the Chariot* by Patrick White, by kind permission of Jonathan Cape Ltd: and the quotation on p. 204 is taken from 'I Remember, I Remember' in Philip Larkin's collected poems *The Less Deceived*, by kind permission of the Marvell Press.

Photographic Acknowledgements
Shirley Conran's photograph on page 6 was taken by Jonathan Player, and Patric Walker's photograph on page 7 was taken by David Smith.

SUPERCONTENTS

SHIRLEY CONRAN

Shirley Conran is the eldest of six children and has two of her own. She trained as a sculptor in Portsmouth, and then studied painting at Chelsea Polytechnic. She worked as a designer for ten years, started Conran Fabrics and has been a judge at the Design Centre. She nipped into journalism as Home Editor of the *Daily Mail* and has also worked as Woman's Editor of the *Daily Mail* and the *Observer*.

In 1974, Shirley turned to the world of books, and wrote *Superwoman*, everywoman's book of household management. It was immediately hailed with a shower of praise as the 'modern Mrs Beeton'. *Superwoman* rapidly became a resounding success round the world.

Superwoman accurately reflects Shirley Conran's philosophy for running a home while pursuing many other interests. She explains: '*Superwoman* is based on 20 years' experience of industry and housework.

'I make no secret of the fact that I would rather lie on a sofa than dust underneath it – but you have to be efficient if you are going to be lazy.

'What *Superwoman* does is show you how to save time in the home and what to do with the time you save. It helps you to do the work you don't like as fast as possible.

'It is for the women who have to housekeep – but might prefer to do something else.'

PATRIC WALKER

Patric Walker is Britain's leading astrologer, predicting the futures of *Daily Mirror* readers. He also writes the stars for *Woman's Journal* and in the United States for *Town and Country* and *New Woman*. Dark, suave, funny and charming, he is known for his uncanny accuracy and the unusual precision of his prophecies – with no woolly predictions about meeting a tall, dark stanger some time in the future. He says:

'There is nothing magic about astrology. Anyone can learn it if they can use simple arithmetic.

'Perhaps the growing interest in astrology is because people are feeling unprotected; they feel no one is in control of them or responsible for them.

'They are questioning religious beliefs, dogmas and doctrines. They are finding that astrology is more sensible than they thought and that it isn't so unbending, unbelievable or demanding as other beliefs. The least thing you can say about astrology is that there has never been a religious war about it.

'The basic fear in life is fear of the unknown. Astrology is not concerned with the after-life; it is optimistically concerned with present life and living it to the full.

'What the stars do is show your potential; they are not fatalists. They show not what is *going to happen*, but what might easily happen if you don't watch out.

'You are left with free will, with choice. The birth chart is like an unworked tapestry. It's already blocked out and your choice is in colour, texture and contrast. It's all *petit point*.

'But being left with free will, how many want to face their faults? And how many can? It's difficult enough to face the truth and most difficult of all to tell it to oneself.

'I believe that whatever mess we make of our lives, a good 60 per cent we make ourselves.

'Your life is a matter of timing and mistiming. You know when you've mistimed something, when you've forced the situation and told someone the truth at the wrong time or in the wrong way for their temperament to accept.

'For instance, you should approach a Piscean differently from a Virgoan. A Piscean will approach a problem emotionally, whereas a Virgoan will approach it clinically, rationally.

'Certainly your characteristics are inherited from your parents and all those other ancestors and are not entirely dependent on when your parents got together.

'But I think it is within all of us to deny fate, to take life by the throat and shake it and to use our lives to the full.'

OLD FRIENDS, NEW FRIENDS

(You fill in the telephone numbers)

Police	_____
Hospital	_____
Doctor	_____
Dentist	_____
Chemist	_____
Solicitor	_____
Gas Board	_____
Electricity Board	_____
Fire Brigade	_____
Electrician	_____
Plumber	_____
Carpenter	_____
Decorator	_____
Vet	_____
Laundry	_____
Window Cleaner	_____
Taxi-Cabs	_____
Railway Station	_____
TV Repairs	_____
Telephone Repairs	_____
Garage	_____
Milkman	_____
Town Hall	_____
Library	_____
Bank Manager	_____
Accountant	_____
Insurance Broker	_____
Local Odd Job Agency	_____
School	_____

Name and Address   Telephone

Name   _____

Address   _____

_____

_____

Phone Number   _____

Car or Cycle Number   _____

House Keys Number*   _____

Car Keys Number   _____

Driving Licence Number   _____

National Insurance Number   _____

Family Allowance Number   _____

National Health Service Number   _____

Blood Group   _____

Passport Number   _____

Account Number   _____
(Bank/National Savings)

_____

Premium Bond Numbers   _____

_____

_____

_____

RENEWAL DATES: Driving Licence _____

Road Licence _____

Dog Licence _____

Fire Insurance _____

Life Insurance _____

Car Insurance _____

TV Licence _____

Home Insurance _____

*(But if your address is in this diary and you lose the diary, a burglar could have a key made. So invent your own number code and use it for this section, e.g. add a zero after every third number.)

CHRISTMAS PRESENTS LIST

Given

Received

First – *Cotton*

Second – *Paper*

Third – *Leather*

Fourth – *Silk*

Fifth – *Wood*

Sixth – *Iron*

Seventh – *Wool*

Eighth – *Bronze*

Ninth – *Pottery*

Tenth – *Tin*

Twelfth – *Linen*

Fifteenth – *Crystal*

Twentieth – *China*

Twenty-fifth – *Silver*

Thirtieth – *Pearl or Ivory*

Thirty-fifth – *Coral*

Fortieth – *Ruby*

Forty-fifth – *Sapphire*

Fiftieth – *Gold*

Fifty-fifth – *Emerald*

Sixtieth – *Diamond*

WHAT'S FALLING TO PIECES

Make a list here of odd maintenance jobs to be done. Apart from anything else, you'll feel so virtuous when you look back at the end of the year and see that they all add up to a huge heap of work.

Check your household bills here. You can multiply up to £800 with this Ready Reckoner.

With this calculator you can multiply or divide. It's really two sets of tables, 1–20 table across and 1–40 table lined down the page.

In order to multiply 20 × 36 you run one finger across to the 20 column, the other down to 36 and the answer will be where they meet.

If you're working in £s put a £ sign. If you're working in £s and pence do them separately, then add the two together.

1	2	3	4	5	6	7	8	9	10	11	12	13	14	15	16	17	18	19	20	
2	4	6	8	10	12	14	16	18	20	22	24	26	28	30	32	34	36	38	40	2
3	6	9	12	15	18	21	24	27	30	33	36	39	42	45	48	51	54	57	60	3
4	8	12	16	20	24	28	32	36	40	44	48	52	56	60	64	68	72	76	80	4
5	10	15	20	25	30	35	40	45	50	55	60	65	70	75	80	85	90	95	100	5
6	12	18	24	30	36	42	48	54	60	66	72	78	84	90	96	102	108	114	120	6
7	14	21	28	35	42	49	56	63	70	77	84	91	98	105	112	119	126	133	140	7
8	16	24	32	40	48	56	64	72	80	88	96	104	112	120	128	136	144	152	160	8
9	18	27	36	45	54	63	72	81	90	99	108	117	126	135	144	153	162	171	180	9
10	20	30	40	50	60	70	80	90	100	110	120	130	140	150	160	170	180	190	200	10
11	22	33	44	55	66	77	88	99	110	121	132	143	154	165	176	187	198	209	220	11
12	24	36	48	60	72	84	96	108	120	132	144	156	168	180	192	204	216	228	240	12
13	26	39	52	65	78	91	104	117	130	143	156	169	182	195	208	221	234	247	260	13
14	28	42	56	70	84	98	112	126	140	154	168	182	196	210	224	238	252	266	280	14
15	30	45	60	75	90	105	120	135	150	165	180	195	210	225	240	255	270	285	300	15
16	32	48	64	80	96	112	128	144	160	176	192	208	224	240	256	272	288	304	320	16
17	34	51	68	85	102	119	136	153	170	187	204	221	238	255	272	289	306	323	340	17
18	36	54	72	90	108	126	144	162	180	198	216	234	252	270	288	306	324	342	360	18
19	38	57	76	95	114	133	152	171	190	209	228	247	266	285	304	323	342	361	380	19
20	40	60	80	100	120	140	160	180	200	220	240	260	280	300	320	340	360	380	400	20
21	42	63	84	105	126	147	168	189	210	231	252	273	294	315	336	357	378	399	420	21
22	44	66	88	110	132	154	176	198	220	242	264	286	308	330	352	374	396	418	440	22
23	46	69	92	115	138	161	184	207	230	253	276	299	322	345	368	391	414	437	460	23
24	48	72	96	120	144	168	192	216	240	264	288	312	336	360	384	408	432	456	480	24
25	50	75	100	125	150	175	200	225	250	275	300	325	350	375	400	425	450	475	500	25
26	52	78	104	130	156	182	208	234	260	286	312	338	364	390	416	442	468	494	520	26
27	54	81	108	135	162	189	216	243	270	297	324	351	378	405	432	459	486	513	540	27
28	56	84	112	140	168	196	224	252	280	308	336	364	392	420	448	476	504	532	560	28
29	58	87	116	145	174	203	232	261	290	319	348	377	406	435	464	493	522	551	580	29
30	60	90	120	150	180	210	240	270	300	330	360	390	420	450	480	510	540	570	600	30
31	62	93	124	155	186	217	248	279	310	341	372	403	434	465	496	527	558	589	620	31
32	64	96	128	160	192	224	256	288	320	352	384	416	448	480	512	544	576	608	640	32
33	66	99	132	165	198	231	264	297	330	363	396	429	462	495	528	561	594	627	660	33
34	68	102	136	170	204	238	272	306	340	374	408	442	476	510	544	578	612	646	680	34
35	70	105	140	175	210	245	280	315	350	385	420	455	490	525	560	595	630	665	700	35
36	72	108	144	180	216	252	288	324	360	396	432	468	504	540	576	612	648	684	720	36
37	74	111	148	185	222	259	296	333	370	407	444	481	518	555	592	629	666	703	740	37
38	76	114	152	190	228	266	304	342	380	418	456	494	532	570	608	646	684	722	760	38
39	78	117	156	195	234	273	312	351	390	429	468	507	546	585	624	663	702	741	780	39
40	80	120	160	200	240	280	320	360	400	440	480	520	560	600	640	680	720	760	800	40
1	2	3	4	5	6	7	8	9	10	11	12	13	14	15	16	17	18	19	20	

SIZING THEM UP-Family Sizes

Name _____

Age _____

Height _____

Chest _____

Waist _____

Hips _____

Gloves _____

Socks _____

Shoes _____

Collar _____

Hat _____

Name _____

Age _____

Height _____

Chest _____

Waist _____

Hips _____

Gloves _____

Socks _____

Shoes _____

Collar _____

Hat _____

Name _____

Age _____

Height _____

Chest _____

Waist _____

Hips _____

Gloves _____

Socks _____

Shoes _____

Collar _____

Hat _____

Name _____

Age _____

Height _____

Chest _____

Waist _____

Hips _____

Gloves _____

Socks _____

Shoes _____

Collar _____

Hat _____

Use the space at the end to add items which should be on *your* list . . .

Bakeries
Bread
Rolls
Cakes
Biscuits

Dairy Produce
Eggs
Cheese
Milk
Cream
Soured cream
Yoghurt

Drinks
Tea
Instant coffee
Coffee beans
Chocolate
Cocoa
Beer
Wine
Spirits
Soda water
Minerals
Squash

Fruit
Apples
Bananas
Oranges
Grapefruit
Grapes
Lemons

Fats
Butter
Margarine
Lard
Cooking oil

Meat and Fish
Butcher meat
Cooked meat
Sausages
Bacon
Poultry
Pet foods
Fish

Preserves
Jam
Marmalade
Honey
Treacle/syrup
Redcurrant jelly
Mincemeat

Condiments/Sauces
Salt
Pepper
Mustard
Chutney/pickles
Tomato/brown sauce
Mayonnaise
Mint sauce
Horseradish
Olive oil
Vinegar

Tins/Frozen Foods
Fruit
Vegetables
Soups
Fruit juices
Fish
Meat
Pet foods
Milk

Chemist
Soap
Toothpaste
Lavatory paper
Shampoo
Tissues
Plasters
STs
Razor blades

Vegetables
Beans
Cabbage
Carrots
Cauliflower
Cucumber
Lettuce
Mushrooms
Parsley/mint
Peas
Potatoes
Peppers
Spring onions
Tomatoes

Turnips
Onions

Miscellaneous
Cereals
Flour
Cornflour
Pasta
Rice
Sugar
Dried fruit
Herbs/spices
Bouillon cubes
Yeast
Nuts
Olives
Custard powder

Cleaning Materials
Washing-up liquid
Soap powder
Disinfectant
Bleach
Scouring pads
Polish
Silver/brass cleaners
Dustbin liner bags
Matches

Aluminium foil
Greaseproof paper
Kitchen roll

YOUR OWN LIST

THE SUPERWOMAN SHOPPING GUIDE

We all know that you can waste money by buying too cheaply. It's not the good quality, 'more-than-you-should-have-spent' purchases that you regret, but the bargain substitutes that fall to pieces fast. I write as one who went through 2 beds in my first year of married life, for all the wrong reasons.

This is a guide to good taste, good value and the unusual. In fact it's the cream of British shopping. And it isn't just *my* list, it's the Fleet Street Home Editor's Mafia List.

You can generally get free, *good* advice (and often catalogues) at the addresses listed.

But more important than what's on this list is what's NOT on it. I obviously can't print a guide to bad taste, bad value and the sub-ordinary or I'd be sued more than *Private Eye*. So use this list if you want to be sure of avoiding such disasters as mattresses which only last 6 months, continental quilts full of secondhand feathers about to disintegrate, non-iron items that need ironing and THINGS THAT SHRINK.

It's a London-orientated list because that's where the action is, because that's where the market is and I'm afraid I can't help it.

The list has been checked and is correct at time of going to print.

KEY   One star means expensive. Guess what two stars mean.

BATHROOM

Allied Ironfounders,
28 Brook Street, London W1 (01-499 8941).
Conventional, modern baths in tasteful settings.

* Bonsack Baths,
14 Mount Street, London W1 (01-629 9981).
The ultimate in fibreglass luxury: double, single
and circular baths. Standard range of patterns
includes gold-leaf design. Accessories include
dolphin and seahorse taps – gold or chrome-
plated. Aura of money.

Carron Showroom,
48 Park Lane, London W1 (01-493 4676). Bathroom suites. Discreetly sumptuous. Lots of
colours and variety of bath shapes. Also bathroom furniture.

Evered Supplies,
18 North Audley Street, London W1 (01-499
1845). Exotic and grand. Display Ideal Standard's
luxury baths and soaking tubs among others.
Good for French decorated porcelain; gold fittings.

Habitat,
206–222 Kings Road, London SW3 (01-351
1211); 156–158 Tottenham Court Road, London
W1 (01-388 1721) and branches around the
country. Also mail order service through Habitat
Designs, P.O. Box 25, Wallingford, Oxon.
(Wallingford 35000), where they have a full
showroom and children's playground. Good for
basic bathroom accessories; loo-paper and soap
holders; pretty mugs, towels.

Harrods,
Knightsbridge, London SW1 (01-730 1234). Big bathroom centre; has a Bonsack Boutique within. Baths, suites and all sorts of accessories to be found (covered Kleenex boxes for instance).

Humpherson,
Beaufort House, Holman Road, London SW11 (01-228 8811). Plumbers' merchants and kitchen and bathroom specialists. Lots of bathroom settings; coloured bathroom suites; taps, tiles and advice.

National Federation of Builders' and Plumbers' Merchants,
15 Soho Square, London W1 (01-439 1753). Also houses the National Federation of Roofing Contractors and the National Guild of Architectural Ironmongers. Runs the Home Improvement Centre Scheme and will supply information on local showrooms for bathrooms, kitchens, central heating, glass and double-glazing, etc. This is an advice centre. Best to write for lists.

Pearson Mirrorlite,
P.O. Box 48, North Point, Meadowhall Road, Sheffield (Sheffield 43333). Supply bathroom accessories, notably mirror tiles, to varied trade and retail outlets. No showroom, but will give addresses of nearest stockists.

Renubath,
596 Chiswick High Road, London W4 (01-995 5252). Will re-cover stove enamelled baths in a wide choice of colours.
Efficient service.

Local Town Hall or Council Offices,
for information on improvement grants.

KITCHEN: UNITS

Advance Domestic Appliances,
18 Berners Street, London W1 (01-580 9991). Splendid showroom with twelve kitchen sets each by a different manufacturer in varying degrees of sophistication. Westinghouse and Scholtes equipment, some expensive and very grand but there's now a medium-priced range too.

Glynwed Showroom,
28 Brook Street, London W1 (01-499 8941). Where you should go if you want to buy an Aga. It's the main Aga showroom and the country cook's Mecca. Agas in red, white, dark blue, dark green and cream. Other things on show include kitchen sinks, Vogue bathrooms, boilers, etc.

Harrods,
Knightsbridge, London SW1 (01-730 1234). Has a big selection of English and Continental units, mainly on the grand side. The equipment section has no particular personality and an embarrassment of choice. There can't be much you couldn't find there of the shiny and smart variety if you looked long enough.

* Heal's,
196 Tottenham Court Road, London W1 (01-636 1666). Very good selection of English and Continental kitchens. If you want the expensive and best this is where you'll find it. Good for ceramic tiles. Fitted kitchens and planning service. Equipment section is modern, stylish and well stocked.

John Lewis,
Oxford Street, London W1 (01-637 3434), plus branches: **Peter Jones,** Sloane Square, London SW1 (01-730 3434); **Jones Brothers,** Holloway Road, London N7 (01-607 2727); the new branch at Brent Cross Shopping Centre, London NW4 (01-202 6535); and others round the country. Don't make much effort to create realistic kitchen sets, but there's a good choice of middle-priced units. Cooking equipment cheap and well chosen.

Room For Living,
40 Wigmore Street, London W1 (01-486 3351); 70–80 High Road, Bushey Heath, Herts (01-950 6945); 113–115 New Zealand Avenue, Walton-on-Thames (Walton-on-Thames 41438). Extensive range of kitchen units, including Nieburg from Germany (not shown elsewhere).

John Strand Kitchens,
152–156 Kentish Town Road, London NW1 (01-267 2051). Simple room sets from the middle to cheaper ranges of units. Some fifteen kitchen sets on display.
Planning advice available.

KITCHEN: EQUIPMENT

Richard Dare,
93 Regents Park Road, London NW1 (01-722 9428). Sells traditional and classical kitchen utensils. Collects the goods himself from France. Loves baskets, Provençal pottery and cooking – as you can tell from the practical nature of the shop. Lots of pots and pans and coffee-making machines.

Elizabeth David,
46 Bourne Street, London SW1 (01-730 3123). A very clean-looking shop. Everything for the classic French cuisine, without the personal touch of the owner, who seems to more or less let it run itself.

Tempe Davies,
107 Kentish Town Road, London NW1 (01-485 1258). Two floors of very personal choice which is difficult to fault. Big pine kitchen tables and other pine furniture, some exclusive. Most basic kitchen equipment; garden terracotta, bamboo blinds, hand-blown Spanish glass, Portuguese pottery.

Dickins & Jones,
Regent Street, London W1 (01-734 7070). Opened a kitchen shop downstairs in 1976. Full of let's-go-to-town shopping goods: pretty and not cheap.

Divertimenti,
68 Marylebone Lane, London W1 (01-935 0689). Specializes in traditional French cookware. Now much enlarged with a seemingly endless variety of goods, spiced with odd old museum pieces.

Habitat,
206–222 Kings Road, London SW3 (01-351 1211); 156–158 Tottenham Court Road, London W1 (01-388 1721) and shops around the country. Mail order service through Habitat Designs, P.O. Box 25, Wallingford, Oxon. (Wallingford 35000). Good for basic cookware. Specially for pottery and baskets, glass, casseroles, with a few cookbooks. Knives disappointing. [N.B. Habitat mail order does not handle any breakables.]

Liberty,
Regent Street, London W1 (01-734 1234). Newish crockery shop full of mugs, bowls, jugs and glass. Not expensive but you have to work your way through the rather precious crafts section to find it.

David Mellor,
4 Sloane Square, London SW1 (01-730 4259). Round the corner from Elizabeth David. David Mellor designs and manufactures in Sheffield and sells his own cutlery in the shop. Selective choice of pottery, cutlery (of course), glass, gadgets and Yorkshire biscuits.

Merchant Chandler,
72 New Kings Road, London SW6 (01-736 6141). Everything cheap you might need for the kitchen including crockery, glass, kitchen utensils, baskets. Three or four tiny floors, rather like shopping in a tree trunk.

Modern Kitchen Equipment of Liverpool (run by the brothers Swerdlow), 2 Myrtle Street, Liverpool (051-709 7711). Catering equipment and therefore among the most practical you can get. But also the most aesthetic: Sabatier, Le Creuset and Pearson's to name but a few.

LIVING ROOM

* Aram Designs,
3 Kean Street, Covent Garden, London WC2 (01-240 3933). Italian and the best. Two big floors of old Covent Garden warehouse holds Zeev Aram's personal choice of mainly seating and tables.
Lots of leather. Also lighting.

* Co-Existence,
10 Argyle Street, Bath (Bath 61507). Chairs, tables, cushions, hand-printed fabrics. Everything here is modern with tremendous style. Complete design service and lots to look at.

Habitat,
206–222 Kings Road, London SW3 (01-351 1211); 156–158 Tottenham Court Road, London W1 (01-388 1721) and branches around the country. Mail order services through Habitat Designs, P.O. Box 25, Wallingford, Oxon.

(Wallingford 35000). Good for unit seating, sag bags and a small, carefully controlled selection of carpets. Lots of rugs.

Harrods,
Knightsbridge, London SW1 (01-730 1234). Huge furniture selection with practically everything you are looking for, antique, repro or modern, if you're prepared to walk far enough to see it all. Way In Living (follow the blue lights) is a new addition next to Way In with young, bright, jolly Scandinaviany and surprisingly cheap furniture, cushions, tableware and lots of shelving.

* Heal's,
196 Tottenham Court Road, London W1 (01-636 1666). The nearest thing to a museum of modern furniture in London (except possibly Oscar Woollens). There is also a Heal's in Guildford and Dunns of Bromley is now theirs. You will find the heavily upholstered as well as the moulded.

John Lewis,
Oxford Street, London W1 (01-637 3434). Not just conventional furniture but bamboo and knock-down too. Not just floral, but corduroy and tweed too. And never, of course, knowingly undersold. Same applies to other branches including the one at the new Brent Cross Shopping Centre, London NW4 (01-202 6535), **Jones Brothers,** Holloway Road, London N7 (01-607 2727), and others round the country, not forgetting **Peter Jones,** Sloane Square, London SW1 (01-730 3434), which has an added polite flavour. Shelving, though, is less than splendid.

* Liberty,
Regent Street, London W1 (01-734 1234). Furniture fit for embassies. Modern and antique. A lovely shop to spend money in.

Maples,
191 Brompton Road, Knightsbridge, London SW3 (01-589 8202); 247-257 Euston Road, London NW1 (01-387 7000). Made their big mistake when they gave up selling antiques and making their own repro. Now sell modern and other people's repro lines – a mixed bag of the grand and the cheap. Have 50 branches around the country.

Selfridges,
Oxford Street, London W1 (01-629 1234). The common denominator. Plenty to choose from but not shouting with personality.

* Oscar Woollens,
421 Finchley Road, London NW3 (01-435 7750). Come here for the cream of European furniture. Film companies get their smart sets made up here. The accent is on Italian. Good selection of Scandinavian. A show flat at Pier House, Albert Bridge, is also open to the public.

DINING ROOM

* Artesania,
507 Kings Road, London SW10 (01-352 9187). Spanish-made furniture in the Sicilian style imported from little villages outside Madrid. Solid, rather heavy, well suited to dining rooms.

Tempe Davies,
107 Kentish Town Road, London NW1 (01-485 1258). Will have pine tables made to order. Will make heavy pine furniture to customers' own designs: tables, dressers, sideboards, etc.

* Harrods,
Knightsbridge, London SW1 (01-730 1234). As always, if you look hard enough you'll probably find it; from the grand to the simple. Way In Living has the 'youngest' things, and the cheapest prices.

* Heal's,
196 Tottenham Court Road, London W1 (01-636 1666). Round, oblong, circular, square, extending tables in many modern forms and many choices of wood. From all over the Continent, excellent quality and not cheap.

* Liberty,
Regent Street, London W1 (01-734 1234). Dining is the métier of this shop. Elegant and strong boards, ready for groaning, with suitable seating, of course.

The Scandinavian Room,
Gees Court, 77 New Bond Street, London W1 (01-688 1993) and branches. Tweedy, teaky, good tasty Scandinavian.

* Oscar Woollens,
421 Finchley Road, London NW3 (01-435 7750). The grand, the beautiful, the designed, mostly from Italy.

BEDROOMS

Aeonics,
92 Church Road, Mitcham, Surrey (01-640 1113) and 291 Finchley Road, London NW3 (01-794 7257). Man-made fibre or feather-and-down filled duvets; kits for duvets; duvet covers. (The kits aren't all that much cheaper.) Eiderdown-into-duvet service.

Barkers,
Kensington High Street, London W8 (01-937 5432). Have taken over Pontings and have excellent linen department in the basement. Specially good for bargain linen sheets.

British Home Stores,
252–258 Oxford Street, London W1 (01-629 2011) and stores in most major towns. Sell polyester and cotton sheets in pastels and deep colours. Flannelette in winter. Usual floral designs. Duvets, valances, etc. too.

* German Bedding Centre,
Karo-Step, 138 Marylebone Road, London NW1 (01-935 0196). Traditional continental quilts, which are expensive and beautiful. Will also clean and recondition eiderdowns, quilts and duvets.

Habitat,
206–222 Kings Road, London SW3 (01-351 1211); 156–158 Tottenham Court Road, London W1 (01-388 1721), and branches around the country. Mail order service through Habitat Designs, P.O. Box 25, Wallingford, Oxon. (Wallingford 35000). Bright cotton sheets and duvet covers. Super basic blanket. Wool blankets too.

* Harrods,
Knightsbridge, London SW1 (01-730 1234). Marvellous choice of beds, both repro and modern, grand and small. Largest linen department in the country. Linen sheets in three qualities; also cotton, polyester/cotton and silk.

* Heal's,
196 Tottenham Court Road, London W1 (01-636 1666). Make own beds to order to customers' specifications. Also sell Relyon, Sleepeezee, Slumberland, Vono, Meyer and Lattoflex. Advice leaflets on buying bedding upstairs. Lots of divans and pretty headboards. Linen department smallish but imaginative.

John Lewis,
Oxford Street, London W1 (01-637 3434); also **Peter Jones,** Sloane Square, London SW1 (01-730 3434); **Jones Brothers,** Holloway Road, London N7 (01-607 2727); the new branch at Brent Cross Shopping Centre, London NW4 (01-202 6535); and other branches round the country. Good selection of beds and sofa beds at good prices. Also Jonelle sheets (sheeting now in prints), duvets and covers.

Limericks,
110 Hamlet Court Road, Westcliff-on-Sea, Essex (Westcliff-on-Sea 43486). Sells everything for the linen cupboard by mail order. Catalogue is full of double damasks, sheeting, candlewick, linen, window cleaners' scrim, etc.

The Linen Cupboard,
21–22 Great Castle Street, London W1 (01-629 4062). Good bargains in sheets and towels by best-known British firms and some expensive flowery American sheets; blankets, table and bath linen.

The Linen Tree,
62 South Audley Street, London W1 (01-629 0223). All sorts of sheets, linen, cotton, polyester/cotton – mostly American. Matching bed sets and towels.

The London Bedding Centre,
26 Sloane Street, London SW1 (01-235 7542). Relyon, Sleepeezee, Slumberland, Bi-Spring, Staples, etc. Advice leaflets. Small amount of bedding upstairs.

* Maples,
247–257 Euston Road, London NW1 (01-387 7000); 191 Brompton Road, Knightsbridge, London SW3 (01-589 8202) and branches. Beds, storage and bedding. Mostly the rather traditional grand.

Marks & Spencer,
Two big branches in Oxford Street, London
W1, at Marble Arch (01-935 7954) and by
Oxford Circus (01-734 4904), plus branches. Co-
ordinated blankets, sheets, pillowcases and
duvets, which all in turn co-ordinate with curtains, rugs and wallpapers. Prints and pastels.
Deep colours too. All polyester/cotton. Prints
rather pedestrian.

* National Linen Company,
20 Brook Street, London W1 (01-629 5000).
Finest linen and cotton with a few polyester/cot-
ton. Go there for hand-embroidery.

Room For Living,
40 Wigmore Street, London W1 (01-486 3351);
70–80 High Road, Bushey Heath, Herts (01-950
6945); 113–115 New Zealand Avenue, Walton-
on-Thames, Surrey (Walton-on-Thames 41438).
Fitted storage showroom – mostly white and
clean but choice of put-it-together-yourself or
fairly grand.

Selfridges,
Oxford Street, London W1 (01-629 1234). Selection of most popular beds. Usual selection of
well-known makes of sheets in polyester/cotton.
Good for eiderdowns and blankets.

* The White House,
51-52 New Bond Street, London W1 (01-629
3521). Exquisite linen and cotton and hand-
embroidered sheets and pillowcases. This is
where the Arabs come – it's the best. Has the
largest variety of stock in the UK.

CHILDREN

ESA Creative Learning,
Pinnacles, P.O. Box 22, Harlow, Essex (Harlow
21131). Have educational toys and the kind of
bookcases, trolleys, tables, etc. used in nursery
and primary schools. Have begun to sell play
equipment and Abbatt toys through private
coffee mornings, etc., a bit like Tupperware.

Frog Hollow;
15 Victoria Grove, London W8 (01-584 5645). A
newish shop selling children's 'personalized' pillowcases and duvet covers (3 days from order-

ing); Snoopy bedlinen, big soft toys, cushions,
fabrics and wallpapers for children's rooms.
Exquisite children's clothes.

* Harrods,
Knightsbridge, London SW1 (01-730 1234). Sell
frilly cots and swing cradles and babies' and
children's wear. Also bunks, etc. Their Way In
Living department has lots of furniture suitable
for kids' rooms.

John Lewis,
Oxford Street, London W1 (01-637 3434). Has a
nursery department with cradles and prams and
playgroup sort of toys. Most of their branches
stock similar but smaller range. Their Daniel
Neal shops in Bournemouth and Cheltenham
specialize in nurseryware and school clothes.

Merchant Chandler,
72 New Kings Road, London SW6 (01-736
6141). Sell Moses Baskets and have cradles and
some children's chairs and table units in from
time to time.

Mothercare,
461 Oxford Street, London W1 (01-629 6621)
and branches in most of the major cities and
towns. Sell cheap and some far from boring
clothes – up to 10 years. Mothercare-by-Post at
Cherry Tree Road, Watford, Herts. (Watford
33577) has the full range. Cheapest way to buy
baby gear: prams, baby baskets, baths, etc.
Disposable nappy service. Will send catalogue.

Selfridges,
Oxford Street, London W1 (01-629 1234). Sell a
selection of cots, bunk beds, scaled down chairs
and tables, little wicker chairs, playpens and
something called a 'dresserette'; high chairs;
good selection of prams, pushchairs and travelling cots.

LIGHTING

* Aram Designs,
3 Kean Street, Covent Garden, London WC2
(01-240 3933). Designs by Flos and Arteluce of
Italy. What is in the catalogue but isn't in the
showroom can be produced from the warehouse
a few streets away.

British Home Stores,
252–258 Oxford Street, London W1 (01-629 2011) and stores throughout the country. Already renowned for versatile and modern lighting including track, spot, table and rise-and-fall lamps.

* Co-Existence,
10 Argyle Street, Bath (Bath 61507). Large and super collection of British and European lighting from Artemide, Flos, Sirrah, Verre Lumière etc.

Concord Lighting International,
Rotaflex House, 241 City Road, London EC1 (01-253 1200). Big showroom of the many kinds of spot, track, recessed, etc. lights made by this firm. Advice in the showroom but you can't actually buy from there.

Habitat,
206–222 Kings Road, London SW3 (01-351 1211); 156–158 Tottenham Court Road, London W1 (01-388 1721) and branches. Small but buyable range of modernly tasteful table, standard and pendant lamps. Also perspex, enamel and steel lamps, hessian shades. Not expensive.

Harrods,
Knightsbridge, London SW1 (01-730 1234). Way In Living department has lots of table lamps, modern, amusing and above all cheap.

Heal's,
196 Tottenham Court Road, London W1 (01-636 1666). Rich and rare. All modern lighting. No reproductions. Lots of chrome and brass.

John Lewis,
Oxford Street, London W1 (01-637 3434) and branches. Fairly conventional fittings but a good variety and as cheap as you'll get anywhere.

London Lighting Company,
173 Fulham Road, London SW3 (01-589 4270). Mostly British with a smattering of Japanese and Continental. Lots of clever little reading lamps, spotlights, dip lights, recess lights.

Reject Shop,
245–249 Brompton Road, London SW3 (01-584 7613). Very good choice of lighting for a small department. Discontinued lines, discount items – but all electrically OK, and cheap. Also branches at 209 Tottenham Court Road, London W1 (01-580 2895) and 62–63 East Street, Brighton, Sussex (Brighton 202161).

Ryness,
37 Goodge Street, London W1; 326 Edgware Road, London W2; 67 Camden High Street, London NW1 (01-637 8805 – same for all shops). Electrical shops with huge selection of fittings and switches and small reading lamps of the telescopic and folding variety. Spotlights, dimmer switches, concealed lights, recess lighting.

Christopher Wray's Lighting Emporium,
600–602 Kings Road, London SW6 and his Lamp Workshop, 613–615 Kings Road, London SW6 (01-736 8008 for both). Also his Tiffany Shop along the Kings Road at number 593 (01-731 3633). Sells mostly British with smattering of Continental. Specializes in paraffin lamps.

* Oscar Woollens,
421 Finchley Road, London NW3 (01-435 7750). Sells the grand, modern, exotic and expensive. Mostly Italian lamps. Also Philippine-shell lamps made in Switzerland – very expensive and beautiful.

FLOORING: CARPETS

Afia Carpets,
81 Baker Street, London W1 (01-935 0414). Possibly the best service in London. Quick, helpful, knowledgeable; imaginative selection. Bathroom carpets, some with games on for children, and now a new kitchen carpet from America.

Byzantium,
1 Goodge Street, London W1 (01-636 6465). For inexpensive Greek floor rugs in wool and mixtures.

Carpets International,
14–15 Berners Street, London W1 (01-580 8776). A showroom for CMC, Crossley, Kossett, Gilt Edge, Harington and Illingworth, offering the widest range and among the best in British-made carpeting and soft floorcovering products. Advice, including fitting and laying techniques, care and maintenance, etc.

Heal's,
196 Tottenham Court Road, London W1 (01-636 1666). Scandinavian-type rugs and shaggy pile carpets from New Zealand. Lots of less shaggy too. Don't look here for the traditional patterned carpet.

John Lewis,
Oxford Street, London W1 (01-637 3434) and **Peter Jones,** Sloane Square, London SW1 (01-730 3434). Have their own brand of Wilton carpets called Jonelle Firm Twist; Jonelle Super Twist, Jonelle Sloane, Jonelle Cavendish. Also a design-award-winning range in browns and beiges called Good Companions by Broadloom Carpets.

* Liberty,
Regent Street, London W1 (01-734 1234). Have a carpet-weaving service which is frightfully expensive and takes about 6 weeks.

Queensway Discount Warehouses,
Head Office: Norfolk Tower, Surrey Street, Norwich, Norfolk (Norwich 60277). Main London branches at Cowley Road, The Vale, Acton, London W3 (01-749 6961) and Lee Valley Trading Estate, North Circular Road, Edmonton, London N18 (01-807 3717); also branches around the country. Have carpets specially made for them in five basic colourways. Most carpets heavily patterned, but not all. Fairly conventional, but cheap.

Rooksmoor Mills,
Bath Road, Nr Stroud, Gloucestershire (Amberley 2577). Big showroom of furniture (very good for cane) and good choice of rush and maize matting. Carpets sold include stain-proof and everlasting 'Magic' carpet; Cabash carpets; sisal. Mail order catalogue.

Sapphire Carpets,
14-16 Uxbridge Road, London W4 (01-579 2323) and branches. Used to sell ex-exhibition carpets. Now have a selection of cheap new carpeting. Also bedding and furniture.

Servicemaster,
3 Hammersmith Road, London W6 (01-602 4411). Carpet cleaning service. Also branches throughout the country.

FLOORING: CORK AND VINYL

* Amtico,
Celanese House, 22 Hanover Square, London W1 (01-629 6258). The most interesting, best quality and most expensive vinyl tiles you can get.

Armstrong Cork,
Chequers Square, Uxbridge, Middlesex (Uxbridge 51122). Don't have a showroom in London but they sell their vinyls, tiles, cushion tiles and sheet to multiple stores such as John Lewis.

Wicanders,
41-42 Berners Street, London W1 (Showroom only: 01-636 5959). Floor or wall cork in sheets or tiles. Many colours and patterns including PVC covered cork floor tiles.

Your local DIY shop and department stores will have a selection of vinyl tiles for kitchen or bathroom including Nairn, Marley, etc.

CERAMIC TILES

The Building Centre,
26 Store Street, London WC1 (Information: 01-637 4522). Have a permanent and changing exhibition of building materials, with ceramics on the ground floor.

Ceramica Italia,
115 Crawford Street, London W1 (01-487 5728). Lots of different prices; designs for floors and walls.

Kenneth Clark Pottery,
10a Dryden Street, London WC2 (01-836 1660). Handmade, very individual tiles; wall panels.

Domus,
260 Brompton Road, London SW3 (01-589 9457). Superb tiles from Italy, superbly exhibited . . .

H & R Johnson-Richards,
Ceramic Tile Showroom, 303-306 High Holborn, London WC1 (01-242 0564). Have a

range of glazed and unglazed slip-resistant tiles and special tiles for swimming pools, as well as a large selection of quite pretty tiles for kitchens and bathrooms.

Pilkington's & Carter,
42 Bloomsbury Street, London WC1 (01-580 0941). Looks like somebody's home, but inside is a big showroom with all tiles on display. Showroom only.

Mr Stone's Flooring & Tiling Shop,
90 Muswell Hill Broadway, London N10 (01-883 8879). Has a good selection of well-displayed tiles and an unusually efficient and courteous service.

The Tile Mart,
151 Great Portland Street, London W1 (01-580 3814): 107 Pimlico Road, London SW1 (01-730 7278), and several other branches. Big selection of both English and Continental floor and wall tiles. Not cheap.

DECORATING AND WALLCOVERINGS

Laura Ashley,
40 Sloane Street, London SW1 (01-235 9728). Prettily floral, milkmaidy fabrics and papers for the home. Cheap – not particularly washable.

Coles,
18 Mortimer Street, London W1 (01-580 1066). Old family firm. Hand-printed wallpapers (some untrimmed). Distinguished designs including a range of washable Portuguese tile patterns – good for bathrooms. Good paint range recently brought up to date.

* Designers Guild,
277 Kings Road, London SW3 (01-351 1271). Window-shopper-stopping showroom. Own mainly small print, fresh-looking fabric and papers. Room sets; cushions in own fabrics; advice.

* Elizabeth Eaton,
25a Basil Street, London SW3 (just behind Harrods) (01-589 3281). Well-established and pleasant to go into. Hundreds of 'up-market'

wallpapers – don't go there for Sanderson and Crown. Also good tile section. Room sets and very pretty window.

** David Hicks, Mary Fox Linton,
35 Elystan Street, London SW3 (01-584 4803). Very David Hicks. Geometric and small French-type prints in delicate colours. Also delightfully pretty fabrics. Lots of rather expensive ashtrays and other little accessories.

Home Decorating (Wallpapers),
83 Walton Street, London SW3 (01-584 7927). Superb range of mainly Continental wallpapers (Belgian, Dutch, Swedish) run by two elderly ladies of personality who will give good advice.

Osborne & Little,
304 Kings Road, London SW3 (01-353 1456). Hand-printed, stylish papers. A range of metallic vinyls. Bold designs, excellent colours. Special Swedish papers. Some papers need to be trimmed.

Sanderson,
56 Berners Street, London W1 (01-636 7800). Sort of supermarket cash and carry for all their wallpapers and paints. Matching fabrics and wallcoverings can be seen upstairs. Other co-ordinating departments such as lighting and carpeting.

* John Siddeley (Lord Kenilworth),
4 Harriet Street, London SW1 (01-235 8757). Basically a designer of *House and Garden* style. Excellent selection of American wallpapers.

Mr Stone's Paint & Wallpaper Shop,
175 Muswell Hill Broadway, London N10 (not quite opposite his flooring shop) (01-444 9562). Practically every wallpaper and covering available, both British and foreign, including hessians, grasspapers, felts, etc. Small range of own wallpapers by young British designers. Good service.

Wallpaper Warehouses,
105 Church Street, London NW8 (01-723 4573); 32 Willesden Lane, London NW6 (01-624 1918); also at 34 Willesden Lane (01-328 0487). Bargain prices on mainly Crown and Sanderson papers; Vymura too.

IMPORTANT REGIONAL THEATRES

	Box Office
Bath	
Theatre Royal, Saw Close	Bath 3700
Belfast	
Arts Theatre, 41 Botanic	
Avenue, Belfast 7	Belfast 29167
Birmingham	
Alexandra, Station Street,	
Birmingham B5 4DS	021-643 1231
Repertory Theatre, Broad	
Street, Birmingham B1 2EP	021-236 4455
Bournemouth	
Playhouse, Hinton Road	Bournemouth 23275
Bradford	
Alhambra, Morley Street	Bradford 27007
Brighton	
Dome, Royal Pavilion Estate	Brighton 682127
Theatre Royal, New Street	Brighton 28488
Bristol	
Colston Hall, Colston Street,	
Bristol 1	Bristol 22957
Little Theatre, Colston Street,	
Bristol 1	Bristol 21182
Theatre Royal, King Street,	
Bristol 1	Bristol 24388
Cambridge	
Arts Theatre, Peas Hill	Cambridge 52000
Canterbury	
Marlowe Theatre,	
St Margaret's Street	Canterbury 64747
Cardiff	
New, Park Place	Cardiff 32446
Sophia Gardens Pavilion	Cardiff 27657

Chichester	
Festival Theatre, Oaklands Park	
	Chichester 86333
Coventry	
Belgrade, Corporation Street	Coventry 20205
Croydon	
Fairfield Halls, Park Lane,	
CR9 1DG	01-688 9291
Derby	
Playhouse, Theatre Walk,	
Eagle Centre	Derby 363275
Dundee	
Repertory Theatre, Lochee Road	
	Dundee 26061
Edinburgh	
King's Theatre, Leven Street,	
Edinburgh EH3 9LQ	031-229 1201
Royal Lyceum, Grindlay Street,	
Edinburgh EH3 9AX	031-229 1231
Traverse, 112 West Bow,	
Grassmarket, Edinburgh	
EH1 2PD	031-226 2633
Exeter	
Northcott, John Stocker Road	Exeter 54853
Glasgow	
Citizens', Gorbals Street,	
Glasgow G5 9DS	041-429 0022
Kelvin Hall, Kelvin Grove,	
Glasgow G3 8AW	041-334 1185
King's, Bath Street, Glasgow	
G2 4JN	041-552 5961
Glyndebourne	
Festival Opera, Glyndebourne,	
Lewes, Sussex	Ringrow 812411

Guildford
Yvonne Arnaud Theatre,
Millbrook　　　　　　　Guildford 60191

Hull
New, Kingston Square　　　Hull 20463

Leatherhead
Thorndike Theatre,
Church Street　　　　Leatherhead 77677

Leeds
Grand, New Briggate, Leeds 1　Leeds 40971
City Varieties Music Hall,
The Headrow, Leeds 1　　Leeds 30808
Playhouse, Calverley Street,
Leeds 2　　　　　　　　Leeds 42111

Liverpool
Playhouse Theatre, Williamson
Square, Liverpool 1　　051-709 8363
Royal Court Theatre, Roe
Street, Liverpool 1　　051-709 5163
Philharmonic Hall, Hope Street,
Liverpool 1　　　　　051-709 3789

Manchester
Free Trade Hall, Peter Street,
Manchester M2 3NQ　　061-834 0943
Library Theatre, St Peter's
Square, Manchester M2 5PD　061-236 9422
Opera House, Quay Street,
Manchester 3　　　　061-834 1787
University Theatre, Devas
Street, Manchester M15 6JA　061-273 5696

Newcastle upon Tyne
Theatre Royal, Grey Street
　　　　Newcastle upon Tyne 22061

Nottingham
Playhouse, Wellington Circus,
Nottingham NG1 5AS　Nottingham 45671
Theatre Royal, Parliament Street
　　　　　　　　　Nottingham 42328

Oldham
Coliseum Theatre, Fairbottom
Street　　　　　　　061-624 2829

Oxford
New Theatre, George Street　Oxford 44544
Playhouse, Beaumont Street　Oxford 47133

Richmond (Surrey)
Richmond Theatre, The Green　01-940 0088

Sheffield
Crucible, 55 Norfolk Street,
Sheffield S1 1DA　　　Sheffield 79922

Southampton
Nuffield, University of
Southampton　　　Southampton 555028

Stoke-on-Trent
Victoria Theatre, Hartshill Road,
Hartshill　　　　Stoke-on-Trent 615962

Stratford-on-Avon
Royal Shakespeare Theatre
　　　　　　Stratford-on-Avon 2271

Sunderland
Empire, High Street　　Sunderland 73766

Windsor
Theatre Royal, Windsor　Windsor 61107

York,
Theatre Royal, St Leonard's
Place　　　　　　　　York 23568

LONDON THEATRES

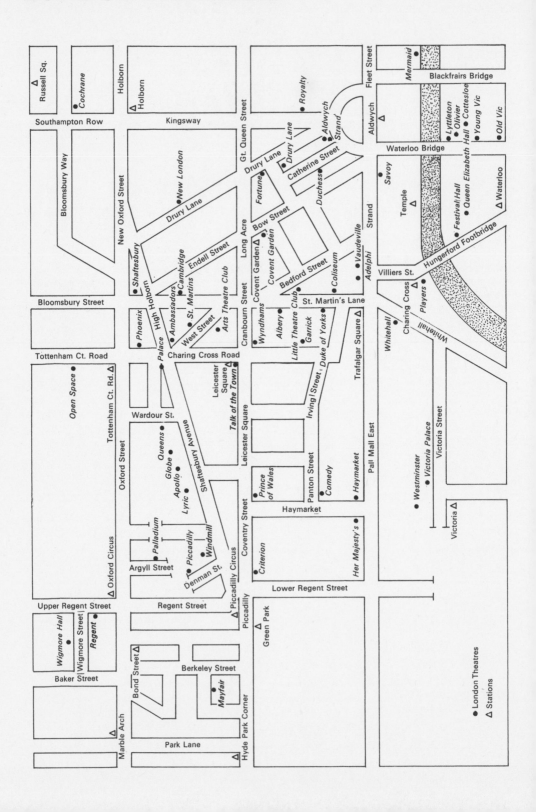

	Box office
Adelphi, Strand, WC2	01-836 7611
Albery, St Martin's Lane, WC2	01-836 3878
Aldwych, Aldwych, WC2	01-836 6404
Ambassadors, West Street, WC2	01-836 1171
Apollo, Shaftesbury Avenue, W1	01-437 2663
Arts, Gt Newport Street, WC2	01-836 3334
Cambridge, Earlham Street, WC2	01-836 6056
Cochrane, Theobalds Road, WC1	01-242 7040
Coliseum, St Martin's Lane, WC2	01-836 7666
Comedy, Panton Street, SW1	01-930 2578
Covent Garden, Covent Garden, WC2	01-240 1066
Criterion, Piccadilly Circus, W1	01-930 3216
Drury Lane, Catherine Street, WC2	01-836 8108
Duchess, Catherine Street, WC2	01-836 8243
Duke of York's, St Martin's Lane, WC2	01-836 5122
Fortune, Russell Street, WC2	01-836 2238
Garrick, Charing Cross Road, WC2	01-836 4601
Globe, Shaftesbury Avenue, W1	01-437 1592
Greenwich, Crooms Hill, SE10	01-858 7755
Greenwood, 55 Weston Street, SE1	01-403 0592
Hampstead, Swiss Cottage Centre, NW3	01-722 9301
Haymarket, Haymarket, SW1	01-930 9832
Her Majesty's, Haymarket, SW1	01-930 6606
King's Head, 115 Upper Street, N1	01-226 1916
Kings Road, 279 Kings Road, SW3	01-352 7488
Little Theatre Club, Long Acre, WC2	01-240 0660
Lyric, Shaftesbury Avenue, W1	01-437 3686
Mayfair, Stratton Street, W1	01-629 3036
Mermaid, Puddle Dock, EC4	01-248 7656
National, (Lyttleton, Olivier, and Cottesloe) South Bank, SE1	01-928 2033
New London, Drury Lane, WC2	01-405 0072
Old Vic, Waterloo Road, SE1	01-928 7616
Open Space, 32 Tottenham Court Road, W1	01-580 4970
Palace, Cambridge Circus, W1	01-437 6834
Palladium, Argyll Street, W1	01-437 7373
Phoenix, Charing Cross Road, WC2	01-836 8611
Piccadilly, Denman Street, W1	01-437 4506
Players, Hungerford Arches, Villiers Street, WC2	01-839 1134
Prince of Wales, Coventry Street, W1	01-930 8681
Queen Elizabeth Hall, Belvedere Road, SE1	01-928 3191
Queens, Shaftesbury Avenue, W1	01-734 1166
Regent, Upper Regent Street, W1	01-323 2707
Roundhouse, Chalk Farm Road, NW1	01-267 2564
Royal Court, Sloane Square, SW1	01-730 1745
Royalty, Portugal Street, WC2	01-405 8004
Royal Festival Hall, Belvedere Road, SE1	01-928 3191
St Martin's, West Street, WC2	01-836 1443
Savoy, Strand, WC2	01-836 8888
Shaftesbury, Shaftesbury Avenue, WC2	01-836 6596
Shaw, Euston Road, NW1	01-388 1394
Strand, Aldwych, WC2	01-836 2660
Theatre Royal, Stratford East, Angel Lane, Stratford, E15	01-534 0310
Vaudeville, Strand, WC2	01-836 9988
Victoria Palace, Victoria Street, SW1	01-834 1317
Westminster, 12 Palace Street, WC2	01-834 0283
Whitehall, Whitehall, SW1	01-930 6692
Windmill, Great Windmill Street, W1	01-437 6312
Wyndham's, Charing Cross Road, WC2	01-836 3028
Young Vic, The Cut, SE1	01-928 6363
Talk of the Town, Hippodrome Corner, WC2	01-734 5051

THE LONDON UNDERGROUND

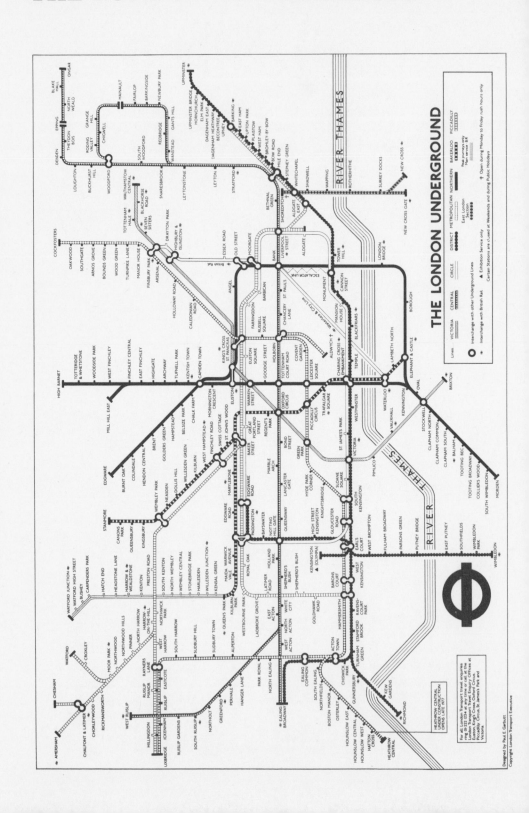

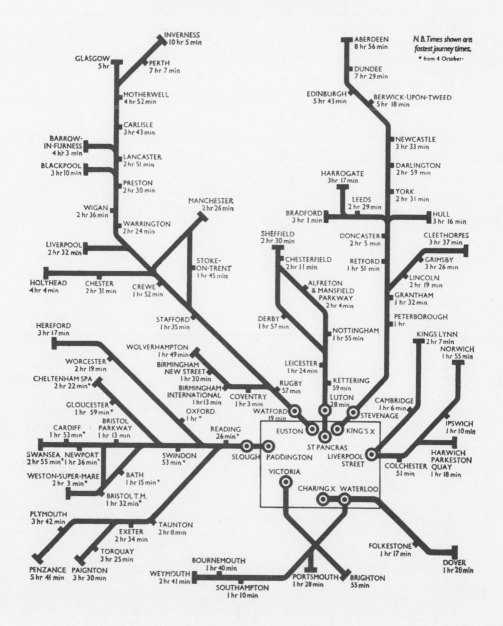

N.B. Times shown are fastest journey times.
* from 4 October *

INVERNESS 10 hr 5 min

GLASGOW 5 hr

PERTH 7 hr 7 min

MOTHERWELL 4 hr 52 min

CARLISLE 3 hr 43 min

BARROW-IN-FURNESS 4 hr 3 min

LANCASTER 2 hr 51 min

BLACKPOOL 3 hr 10 min

PRESTON 2 hr 30 min

MANCHESTER 2 hr 26 min

WIGAN 2 hr 36 min

WARRINGTON 2 hr 24 min

LIVERPOOL 2 hr 32 min

STOKE-ON-TRENT 1 hr 45 min

HOLYHEAD 4 hr 4 min

CHESTER 2 hr 31 min

CREWE 1 hr 52 min

STAFFORD 1 hr 35 min

HEREFORD 3 hr 17 min

WOLVERHAMPTON 1 hr 49 min

WORCESTER 2 hr 19 min

BIRMINGHAM NEW STREET 1 hr 30 min

CHELTENHAM SPA 2 hr 22 min*

BIRMINGHAM INTERNATIONAL 1 hr 13 min

GLOUCESTER 1 hr 59 min*

COVENTRY 1 hr 3 min

OXFORD 1 hr *

CARDIFF 1 hr 53 min*

BRISTOL PARKWAY 1 hr 13 min

READING 26 min*

SWANSEA 2 hr 55 min*

NEWPORT 1 hr 36 min*

SWINDON 53 min*

SLOUGH

PADDINGTON

WESTON-SUPER-MARE 2 hr 3 min*

BATH 1 hr 15 min*

VICTORIA

BRISTOL T.M. 1 hr 32 min*

PLYMOUTH 3 hr 42 min

TAUNTON 2 hr 11 min

EXETER 2 hr 34 min

TORQUAY 3 hr 25 min

PENZANCE 5 hr 41 min

PAIGNTON 3 hr 30 min

BOURNEMOUTH 1 hr 40 min

WEYMOUTH 2 hr 41 min

SOUTHAMPTON 1 hr 10 min

ABERDEEN 8 hr 56 min

DUNDEE 7 hr 29 min

EDINBURGH 5 hr 43 min

BERWICK-UPON-TWEED 5 hr 18 min

NEWCASTLE 3 hr 33 min

DARLINGTON 2 hr 59 min

HARROGATE 3 hr 17 min

LEEDS 2 hr 29 min

YORK 2 hr 31 min

BRADFORD 3 hr 1 min

HULL 3 hr 16 min

SHEFFIELD 2 hr 30 min

DONCASTER 2 hr 5 min

CLEETHORPES 3 hr 37 min

CHESTERFIELD 2 hr 11 min

RETFORD 1 hr 51 min

GRIMSBY 3 hr 26 min

ALFRETON & MANSFIELD PARKWAY 2 hr 4 min

LINCOLN 2 hr 19 min

GRANTHAM 1 hr 32 min

DERBY 1 hr 57 min

NOTTINGHAM 1 hr 55 min

PETERBOROUGH 1 hr

LEICESTER 1 hr 24 min

KINGS LYNN 2 hr 7 min

NORWICH 1 hr 55 min

RUGBY 57 min

KETTERING 59 min

LUTON 28 min

CAMBRIDGE 1 hr 6 min

WATFORD 19 min

STEVENAGE

IPSWICH 1 hr 10 min

EUSTON

KING'S X

ST PANCRAS

LIVERPOOL STREET

HARWICH PARKESTON QUAY 1 hr 18 min

COLCHESTER 51 min

CHARING X

WATERLOO

FOLKESTONE 1 hr 17 min

DOVER 1 hr 28 min

PORTSMOUTH 1 hr 28 min

BRIGHTON 55 min

HOLIDAY PAGE

Bank Holidays 1977

England, N. Ireland, Wales

New Year's Day	Saturday, January 1
St Patrick's Day (N. Ireland)	Thursday, March 17
Good Friday (England and Wales)	Friday, April 8
Easter Monday	Monday, April 11
Late Spring Holiday	Monday, June 6
Queen's Jubilee Bank Holiday	Tuesday, June 7
Late Summer Holiday	Monday, August 29
Boxing Day	Monday, December 26
Bank Holiday	Tuesday, December 27

As New Year's Day falls on a Saturday in 1977 we might get an extra day's holiday. However, at the time of going to press no decision had been made on this.

Scotland

New Year's Day	Saturday, January 1
Bank Holiday	Monday, January 3
Good Friday	Friday, April 8
Spring Bank Holiday	Monday, May 2 (Provisional)
Summer Bank Holiday	Monday, August 1
Bank Holiday	Monday, December 26

Republic of Ireland

New Year's Day	Saturday, January 1
St Patrick's Day	Thursday, March 17
Good Friday	Friday, April 8
Easter Monday	Monday, April 11
June Holiday	Monday, June 6
August Holiday	Monday, August 1
St Stephen's Holiday	Monday, December 26

School or College Terms

Winter begins _____ half term _____ ends _____

Spring begins _____ half term _____ ends _____

Summer begins_____ half term _____ ends _____

Family Holiday Dates

Leave home _____ return home _____

Leave home _____ return home _____

Leave home _____ return home _____

Leave home _____ return home _____

Leave home _____ return home _____

Leave home _____ return home _____

Quick Metric Equivalents

All metric calculations are made in units of 10 and are interrelated: *temperature* in degrees; *solid weight* in grammes; *liquid volume* in litres; *length* in metres; *area* in square metres.

Length
(Common use centimetres, metres and kilometres)

1 inch = 2·5 centimetres
1 foot = 30 cm
1 yard = 90 cm
1 mile = 1·6 kilometres
10 millimetres = 1 cm
100 centimetres = 1 metre
1 metre = 39 inches
1,000 metres = 1 km

Weight
(Common use grammes and kilogrammes).

1 oz $\approx$ 25 grammes
1 lb $\approx$ 450 g
2 lb 3 oz $\approx$ 1 kilogram (1,000 g)

Liquid
(Common use millilitres and litres)

1 fl oz = 25 ml
$\frac{1}{4}$ imperial pint (5 fl oz) = 125 ml
(1$\frac{1}{2}$ decilitres)
$\frac{1}{2}$ imperial pint (10 fl oz) = 250 ml (3 dl)
1 imperial pint (20 fl oz) = 500 ml (6 dl)
1 gallon (8 pints) = 4$\frac{1}{2}$ litres
4 tablespoons (2$\frac{1}{2}$ fl oz) = 70 ml
2 tablespoons (1$\frac{1}{4}$ fl oz) = 35 ml
1 tablespoon ($\frac{5}{8}$ fl oz) = 18 ml
1 dessertspoon ($\frac{2}{5}$ fl oz) = 12 ml
1 teaspoon ($\frac{1}{6}$ fl oz) = 6 ml
1000 ml = 1 litre = 1$\frac{3}{4}$ pints
100 litres = 1 hectolitre

For Journeys

1 mile = 1·6 km
3 miles = 4·8 km
5 miles = 8 km
10 miles = 16 km
30 miles = 48 km
50 miles = 80 km
100 miles = 161 km

Fabrics

(Widths are still the same standard sizes as in pre-metrication days, but they are now translated into centimetres)

Width of dress material

35/36 in = 90 cm
44/45 in = 115 cm
48 in = 120 cm
54/56 in = 140 cm
60 in = 150 cm

Width of soft furnishing materials

48/50 in = 122/124 cm

Surface or Area

1 sq cm = 100 sq mm = 0·1550 sq in
1 sq metre = 10,000 sq cm
         = 1·1960 sq yd
1 sq km = 100 hectares = 0·3861 sq mi
Land is measured in hectares. A hectare is $2\frac{1}{4}$ acres.

All metric equivalents are approximate.

Cup and Spoon Equivalents

Ingredients for recipes in some countries are measured by volume rather than weight, using the cup and spoon as basic measurements.

But how much does a cup hold? How many tablespoons are there in a cup?

And how big is a spoon?

Amazingly enough, it depends on the country in which you are standing.

So if you want to translate recipes from one country's measurements into another's, here are your conversion tables.

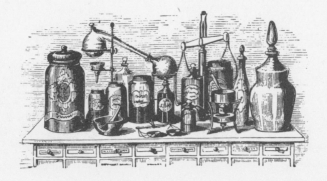

Transatlantic Exchange
(Canada and the United States)

The Easy Way Out

You needn't bother to tax your brain with the following information if, instead, you buy a cheap, simple measuring cone or jug in tin, glass or plastic. Marked on the side, they have all the equivalent measurements you are likely to need for translating transatlantic recipes.

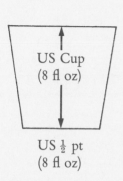

US Cup
(8 fl oz)

US ½ pt
(8 fl oz)

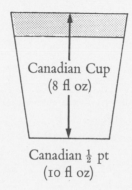

Canadian Cup
(8 fl oz)

Canadian ½ pt
(10 fl oz)

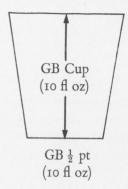

GB Cup
(10 fl oz)

GB ½ pt
(10 fl oz)

Spoons (Solids and liquids)

The British Standard tablespoon and teaspoon are slightly larger than a standard measure tablespoon and teaspoon in the United States and Canada. But on the whole it isn't worth bothering about unless you're measuring something potent – such as strychnine!

Cups (Liquids)

For measuring liquid the same standard cup is used in Canada and the United States and it holds 8 fluid ounces. (Just to make things difficult, this is smaller than the British Standard measuring cup, which holds 10 fluid ounces.)

However, a pint measure in Canada is different from a pint measure in the United States. The Canadians use the British imperial pint, which is 20 fluid ounces. The US pint is smaller – only 16 fluid ounces.

But they both use the 8-ounce standard cup. So . . .

½ US pt = 8 fl oz = 1 cup
1 US pt = 16 floz = 2 cups

½ Canadian pt = 10 fl oz = 1¼ cups
1 Canadian pt = 20 fl oz = 2½ cups

As I've explained already, the British Standard cup = approx. 1¼ US and Canadian cups.

Cup & Spoon Equivalents (continued)

Cups (Solids)

Here is a rough guide of equivalent ingredient measures. They are all based on the North American cup = 8 fl oz = 16 tablespoons.

Table of Equivalents
All measures approximate

Almonds (shelled)	1 lb	3 cups
(coarsely chopped)	1 lb	4 cups
Apples (sliced)	1 lb	3 cups
Baking powder (tartrate)	1 oz	3 tablespoons
Baking powder (phosphate)	1 oz	2½ tablespoons
Bread crumbs (fairly stale)	1 lb	4 cups (packed)
Butter	1 lb	2 cups
	1 oz	2 tablespoons
Cheese (Cheddar or similar)	1 lb	4 cups (grated)
Chocolate (unsweetened)	1 lb	16 squares
	1 oz	1 square (1 tablespoon melted)
Chocolate (unsweetened, grated)	1 oz	5 tablespoons
Citron peel (candied, shredded, lightly packed)	1 lb	4½ cups (approx.)
Cocoa (no sugar added)	1 lb	4 cups (approx.)
Coconut (shredded)	1 lb	6 cups
Coconut (desiccated)	1 lb	4½ cups
Coffee	1 lb	80 tablespoons, 2⅛ cups
Cornflour	1 lb	3 cups
Cottage cheese	1 lb	2 cups
Cream cheese (packaged)	½ lb	1 cup
Currants (dried)	1 lb	3¼ cups
Dates (stoned and chopped)	1 lb	2½ cups
Dried fruit	1 lb	2 cups
Figs	1 lb	3 cups
Flour (unsifted, all-purpose)	1 lb	3½ cups
Flour (sifted, all-purpose)	1 lb	4 cups
	1 oz	4 tablespoons
Gelatine (granulated)	1 oz	2½ tablespoons
Jam	1 oz	1 tablespoon
Lard	1 lb	2 cups
Lemon or orange peel (candied)	1 lb	4 cups (ground, i.e. chopped)
Meat (cooked and ground or chopped)	1 lb	2 cups (packed)
Mustard (ground)	1 oz	7 tablespoons

Nuts: almonds in shells	1 lb	$1\frac{1}{4}$ cups shelled
pecans in shells	1 lb	$1\frac{1}{2}$ cups shelled
peanuts in shells	1 lb	2 cups shelled
walnuts in shells	1 lb	$1\frac{3}{4}$ cups shelled
Oats (rolled)	1 lb	$5\frac{1}{2}$ cups
Peas (split) or lentils	1 lb	2 cups
Raisins	1 lb	3 cups
Rice	1 lb	$2\frac{1}{4}$ cups uncooked
		8 cups cooked
Salt	1 oz	2 tablespoons (approx.)
Spice (ground)	1 oz	4 tablespoons
Suet (chopped)	1 lb	4 cups
	1 oz	$\frac{1}{4}$ cup (approx.)
Sugar		
Brown (depends on moisture)	1 lb	$2\frac{1}{2}$–3 cups firmly packed
Granulated	1 lb	2 cups
	1 oz	2 tablespoons
Castor (also called fruit, berry or powdered sugar)	1 lb	$2\frac{1}{2}$ cups unsifted, $2\frac{3}{4}$ cups sifted
	1 oz	$2\frac{3}{4}$ tablespoons
Icing	1 lb	$3\frac{1}{4}$ cups unsifted $3\frac{1}{2}$ cups sifted
	1 oz	3 tablespoons unsifted
Syrup and honey	1 lb	$1\frac{1}{2}$ cups
	1 oz	1 tablespoon

International Crib

Measure	UK	Australia	New Zealand	Canada	USA
1 pint	20 fl oz	20 fl oz	20 fl oz	20 fl oz	16 fl oz
1 cup	10 fl oz	8 fl oz	8 fl oz	8 fl oz	8 fl oz
1 tablespoon	$\frac{5}{8}$ fl oz	$\frac{1}{2}$ fl oz	$\frac{1}{2}$ fl oz	$\frac{1}{2}$ fl oz	$\frac{1}{2}$ fl oz
1 dessertspoon	$\frac{2}{5}$ fl oz	$\frac{1}{4}$ fl oz	$\frac{1}{4}$ fl oz	not an official measurement	
1 teaspoon	$\frac{1}{5}$ fl oz	$\frac{1}{8}$ fl oz	$\frac{1}{6}$ fl oz	$\frac{1}{6}$ fl oz	$\frac{1}{8}$ fl oz

Cup and Spoon Equivalents

1 UK British Standard cup = $1\frac{1}{4}$ cups in Commonwealth countries and USA

4 UK tablespoons = 5 Commonwealth and 5 US tablespoons

5 UK teaspoons = 6 Canadian, US and New Zealand teaspoons or 8 Australian teaspoons

1 UK dessertspoon = $\frac{2}{3}$ UK tablespoon or 2 UK teaspoons

BASIC COOKERY

All recipes serve 4 unless otherwise stated.

Recipe quantities are given in Imperial and Metric measures. For convenience, metric measures have been rounded off to the nearest 25 grammes, which gives good results in most recipes.

Where pepper is stated I mean freshly ground black pepper. If you haven't got one, buy a pepper mill, it's the professional cook's secret weapon.

Quantity Guide

Most small cream cartons hold a gill ($\frac{1}{4}$ pint/$1\frac{1}{2}$ dl)

A standard mug holds $\frac{1}{2}$ pint/3 dl

Stock

Means bouillon-cube-and-water if you haven't boiled any oxen this week. Don't use Oxo (I don't think Katie has any tastebuds). Buy Knorr Swiss.

How to double boil if you haven't got a boiler

Thick cream sauces and scrambled eggs are better and smoother if made in a double boiler. If you haven't a double boiler cook in a pudding bowl firmly wedged in the top of a saucepan of simmering water. The bowl shouldn't touch the water.

Three things which shouldn't always be kept in the refrigerator

Eggs, soft cheese or cucumber. Use chilled eggs to bake, boil or fry, etc., but you can't use chilled egg whites to beat stiff (for soufflés, meringues and so on) or chilled egg yolks to make a mayonnaise. Soft cheese immediately stops 'working', won't ripen any further and loses its flavour. There's nothing more nastily depressing than a chilled and drooping cucumber.

Cooking frozen vegetables

Ignore the timing instructions on the frozen vegetable packs (they're all different anyway). Simply cook as you do fresh vegetables, that is, until they taste done to you. Like the best heroines, vegetables should be yielding but not too mushy.

ESTABLISHED IN 1780.

WM. BAKER & CO.

PREMIUM CHOCOLATE

COCOA BROMA

DORCHESTER, MASS.

OFFICE 26 SOUTH MARKET STREET, BOSTON, MASS.
AND FOR SALE BY ALL THE PRINCIPAL GROCERS IN THE UNITED STATES.

These articles, to which first Premiums have been awarded by the chief Institutes and Fairs of the Union, are an excellent diet for children, invalids, and persons in health ; allay, rather than induce, the nervous excitement attendant upon the use of tea or coffee, and are recommended by the most eminent physicians. Being manufactured from Cocoa of the best kind and quality, they are warranted equal, if not superior to any other Chocolates made in the United States, and may be returned if found unequal to the recommendation.

AGENTS.

D. C. MURRAY, New York.	KENNETT & DUDLEY, Cincinnati.	LOCKWOOD, WARD & CO., Troy.
GRANT & TWELLS, Phil'a.	WM. BAGALEY & CO., Pittsburg.	VOSE BROTHERS, New Orleans.
THOS. V. BRUNDIGE, Balt.	WAIT & COATES, Albany.	S. H. HOWELL, Georgetown, D. C.

How to translate recipes into metric measures

You can translate recipes into metric measurements working with a weight unit of 25 g ≈ 1 oz (solids) and 1 pint ≈ 575 ml ≈ 6 dl (liquids). The proportion of 25 g solid to 6 dl liquid is the same as the proportion of 1 oz to 1 pint though the total amount in metric is about 10 per cent less.

Recipe Comparisons

25 g	1 oz
100 g	4 oz
1½ dl	¼ pint
3 dl	½ pint
6 dl	1 pint

Oven Temperatures

Solid Fuel	Gas	Electricity (Fahrenheit)	(Centigrade)
Very cool	¼	225° F	110° C
	½	250° F	120° C
Cool	1	275° F	140° C
	2	300° F	150° C
Slow	3	325° F	160° C
Moderate	4	350° F	180° C
	5	375° F	190° C
Moderately hot	6	400° F	200° C
Hot	7	425° F	220° C
Very hot	8	450° F	230° C
	9	475° F	240° C

BASIC RECIPES USED AHEAD

Shortcrust Pastry
(For an 8-inch [21-cm] flan case)

Ingredients
6 oz/175 g plain flour
3 oz/75 g butter cut into sugar-lump size
½ level teaspoon salt
cold water (about 1–1½ teaspoons per oz [25 g] of flour)

Method
1 Sift the flour and salt into a bowl.
2 Cut the butter into the flour and rub in with fingertips until the mixture looks like fine breadcrumbs.
3 Sprinkle a dash of water over the mixture and mix lightly. Repeat until you can draw it together into a soft but not sticky dough.
4 Turn on to a floured board.
5 Knead quickly and lightly into a ball.
6 Roll out with a floured rolling pin or clean empty milk bottle.
7 Bake according to recipe temperatures and times.

When making pastry try to touch the mixture with your fingers as lightly and as little as possible.

White Sauce

Ingredients
½ pint/3 dl milk
1 oz/25 g butter
1 oz/25 g plain flour
salt and pepper

Method
1 Melt the butter in a pan, remove from heat, stir in flour, cook for 2 minutes but do not allow to brown.
2 Gradually add the milk, stirring all the time.
3 Cook and stir until the sauce comes to the boil and thickens.
4 Simmer gently for 2–3 minutes.
5 Season well.
6 If sauce is lumpy, do not despair. Simply whisk in the pan with a beater.

Variations

Lemon Sauce   add juice of half a lemon (good with boiled chicken and rice)

Cheese Sauce   add 3 oz/75 g grated cheese and a dab of French mustard (for serving over cauliflower or leeks)

Egg Sauce   add 1 chopped hardboiled egg and a little chopped parsley (boiled chicken or fish)

Caper Sauce   add 1 teaspoonful capers and a teaspoon of the caper juice (with boiled mutton or white fish)

Tomato Sauce   add 1 tablespoon of tomato purée, twist of lemon peel and bayleaf (good for hardboiled eggs, delicious poured over fish or scallops)

Shrimp Sauce   add 2 oz/50 g unfrozen peeled shrimps, squeeze lemon, lots of pepper and a tablespoon white wine (if possible) (serve with white fish such as cod)

Hot Mustard Sauce   add a good squeeze French mustard and a bayleaf (good with grilled herrings)

Quick Curry Sauce   peel and finely chop a small onion, fry in butter, then proceed as for white sauce, adding 1 teaspoonful of curry powder along with the flour (good with rabbit or chopped remains of Sunday joint)

(Incidentally, to make these sauces into soups, just slowly stir in more hot milk and serve piping hot.)

French Salad Dressing (*Vinaigrette*)

Ingredients
4 tablespoons oil
2 tablespoons white wine vinegar
salt and pepper
1–2 cloves garlic, peeled and crushed
dash of French mustard

Method
1 Beat all ingredients together with a fork or in a blender until *well* mixed.

Increase quantities as necessary. Any leftover vinaigrette will keep in a screw-topped jar for at least a week.

Mayonnaise ($\frac{1}{2}$ pint/3dl)

Ingredients
2 egg yolks
pinch of dry mustard
salt and pepper
$\frac{3}{4}$ cup salad oil
2 tablespoons white wine vinegar

Method
1 Beat egg yolks and seasonings with a wooden spoon or whisk until thick.
2 Add the oil *drop by drop* and by the time you've added 2 tablespoons oil the mixture should be very thick.
3 Carefully stir in 1 teaspoon vinegar and the remaining oil can then be added a little more quickly, beating each time you add more oil.
4 When all the oil has been used, add vinegar and seasoning to taste.
5 If you curdle it, start as above with another egg yolk and seasoning but instead of adding oil, add the curdling mayonnaise, drop by drop.
6 Or buy Hellman's bottled mayonnaise (the best shop-bought one) and disguise it by beating in a squeeze of fresh lemon or a crushed clove of garlic.

Brown Bone Stock

Ingredients
3 lb/1$\frac{1}{4}$ kg beef bones
2 onions, peeled and quartered
2 carrots, peeled and quartered
1 stick celery, cut into pieces
large bouquet garni
6 peppercorns
3 quarts/3$\frac{1}{2}$ litres water
salt

Method
1 Wipe bones, but if possible do not wash.
2 Put bones into your largest pan, with vegetables, herbs, peppercorns and the water, which should come up to about two-thirds above level of bones.
3 Bring slowly to the boil, skimming with spoon when necessary, then half cover pan to allow the liquid to reduce.
4 On lowest possible heat simmer for 4–5 hours, or until stock tastes strong enough. When cold, the stock will set to a jelly-like consistency.

Chicken Stock

Substitute chicken carcass for beef bones. Disguise nauseating smell with 2 tablespoons white wine or white wine vinegar and 2 cloves garlic, peeled and crushed.

Your Menu

My family love reading right through a
menu and picking out three dishes they particularly
want to eat during the coming week.
So I've sorted out these recipes
under menu headings, rather than
alphabetical ones.
It's what I do at home and you may like to try it.

Soups

Light Dishes

(First course, snacks, supper dishes)

Main Dishes

Vegetables

Puddings and Sweets

Teatime

Pickles and Preserves

Sauces and Dips

Drinks

QUICK CALORIE COUNTER

Many diets are planned on a strict control of calories, e.g. you are recommended a thousand calories a day and it appears that you can eat just what you like providing it does not exceed this count. If you do this irrespective of food value you will be eating a badly planned diet, so concentrate on the protein foods. The calories given are average only, particularly when dealing with tinned and ready-prepared goods. As this is a yearly diary we are continuing to use imperial measures first, followed by metric equivalents.

	Average portion	Calories
Beverages and Soft Drinks		
Tea, without milk and sugar	1 cup, 6 fl oz/160 ml	Negligible
Tea, with average amount of milk and 1 teaspoon sugar	1 cup, 6 fl oz/160 ml	75
Coffee, black	1 cup, 6 fl oz/160 ml	Negligible
Coffee, with average amount of milk and 1 teaspoon sugar	1 cup, 6 fl oz/160 ml	85
Cocoa, made with all milk	1 cup, 6 fl oz/160 ml	135
Beef stock cube	1	10–15
Grapefruit/pineapple/orange juice	1 bottle, 4 fl oz/100 ml	70
Tomato juice	1 bottle, 4 fl oz/100 ml	25
Fruit squashes and cordials	wineglass, 4.4 fl oz/125 ml	64–75
Bitter lemon	1 bottle, 6 fl oz/160 ml	56
Slimline bitter lemon	1 bottle, 6 fl oz/160 ml	0.84
Tonic water	1 bottle, 6 fl oz/160 ml	66
Slimline tonic water	1 bottle, 6 fl oz/160 ml	0.84
Coca-cola	1 can, 11·5 fl oz/325 ml	125
Alcoholic Drinks		
Beer: Mild	1 pint/6 dl	140
Bitter	1 pint/6 dl	180
Lager	1 pint/6 dl	150
Stout	1 pint/6 dl	200
Strong Ales	1 pint/6 dl	420
Cider: Dry	1 pint/6 dl	200
Sweet	1 pint/6 dl	240
Vintage	1 pint/6 dl	560
Wines: Red/white/champagne		
Dry	wineglass, 4.4 fl oz/125 ml	90
Sweet	wineglass, 4.4 fl oz/125 ml	115

Spirits

Gin	double measure	110
Whisky	double measure	120
Rum	double measure	150
Vodka	double measure	130

Liqueurs

Brandy and most liqueurs	av. liqueur glass, 1 fl oz/30 ml	75

Nibbles

Peanuts	8 nuts	80
Olives	6 olives	30
Potato crisps	2 oz/50 g	320

Pickles/Sauces

Pickles, sweet	1 tablespoon	50
Mayonnaise, homemade	1 tablespoon	80
Salad dressing	1 tablespoon	100
Tomato ketchup	1 tablespoon	15

Dairy Foods

Cheese: Cheddar and similar	1 medium piece	130
Cream	1 dessertspoon	150
Cottage	1 dessertspoon	40

Cream: double	1 tablespoon	80
single	1 tablespoon	40
Eggs: raw or boiled	1 egg	80
fried	1 egg	140
scrambled	1 tablespoon	250

Fats

Butter	2 small pats	100
Margarine	2 small pats	100
Lard	1 tablespoon	180
Olive oil	1 tablespoon	80

Milk

Fresh, whole	1 pint/6 dl	380
Fresh, skimmed	1 pint/6 dl	200
Condensed and sweetened	1 tablespoon	80

Yoghurt: natural low-fat	5 oz carton/125 g	75
fruit-flavoured	5 oz carton/125 g	125
Ice cream	1 medium tub	100

Soups
(Amount of calories varies greatly according to manufacturer)

Clear	½ pint/3 dl	40–65
Thick	½ pint/3 dl	90–200

Fish

Cod: steamed	1 medium steak	110
fried/		
grilled	1 medium steak	190
Crab	3 tablespoons	150
Haddock:		
steamed	1 medium fillet	84
fried	1 medium fillet	200
smoked steamed	1 medium fillet	110
Lobster	½ medium	100
Mussels	20	75
Oysters	6	40
Plaice: steamed	1 medium	100
fried	1 medium	200
Prawns, shelled	12	180
Shrimps, shelled	20	75
Skate, fried	1 medium steak	300
Sole: steamed	1 medium	90
fried	1 medium	320
Trout, steamed	1 medium	150
Turbot, steamed	1 steak	110
Herrings: baked	1 medium	250
fried	1 medium	300
Kippers, grilled	medium pair	200
Mackerel, fried	1 medium	200
Fish fingers	2 fingers	108
Salmon, tinned	2 tablespoons	140

Meat
(An average amount of fat has been taken into account)

Bacon:		
streaky, fried	3 rashers	300
gammon, fried	1 thick rasher	380
back, fried	3 medium rashers	340
Beef:		
steak, grilled	1 medium	350
sirloin, roast	4 slices	330
steak, stewed	2 tablespoons	200
corned	3 slices	150
Lamb:		
leg, roast	4 slices	250
shoulder, roast	4 slices	290
chop, grilled	1 medium	250
scrag, stewed	2 tablespoons	250

Pork:		
leg, roast	4 slices	300
chop, grilled	1 medium	400
Veal, cutlet, fried	1 medium	190

Offal

Brain, calf's, boiled	2 tablespoons	180
Heart, sheep's baked	1 medium	190
Liver, calf's/lamb's/ox/pig's, fried	2 medium slices	230
Kidney, sheep's, fried	3 medium	200
Sweetbread, stewed	3–4 medium	200
Tripe, stewed	3 tablespoons	180

Ready-prepared meats

Ham, boiled	3 slices	250
Pork pie	1 medium	350
Sausages:		
beef, fried	2 large	250
pork, fried	2 large	280
Scotch egg	1	150
Tongue:		
ox, pickled	3 slices	270
sheep's, stewed	2 tongues	250

Poultry and Game

Chicken: roast	4 slices	150
boiled	4 slices	200
Duck, roast	4 slices	250
Goose, roast	4 slices	270
Grouse, roast	4 slices	160
Hare, stewed	3 tablespoons	240
Pigeon: roast	4 slices	150
stewed	4 slices	140
Pheasant, roast	4 slices	200
Rabbit, stewed	3 tablespoons	100
Turkey, roast	4 slices	170

Fruit
(Stewed fruit includes average amount of sugar)

Apple: eating	1 medium	30
stewed	3 tablespoons	120
Apricots: fresh	3 medium	30
stewed	3 tablespoons	100
Avocado pear	½ medium	100
Banana	1 medium	50
Blackberries	3 tablespoons	100
Cherries: eating	12 cherries	30
stewed	3 tablespoons	120

Gooseberries:

dessert	6 large	40
stewed	3 tablespoons	80
Grapefruit, fresh	½ medium	20
Grapes: black	12 grapes	28
white	12 grapes	34
Melon	1 medium slice	30
Orange	1 medium	40
Peach: fresh	1 medium	40
stewed	2 halves	120
Plums: dessert	3 medium	40
stewed	3 tablespoons	80
Pineapple, fresh	1 medium slice	50

Raspberries:

raw	3 tablespoons	30
stewed	3 tablespoons	150
Rhubarb, stewed	3 tablespoons	50
Strawberries, fresh	6 large	20

Dried Fruits

Apricots, stewed	2 tablespoons	200
Dates	6 dates	130
Figs, stewed	2 tablespoons	150
Raisins	1 tablespoon	70
Sultanas	1 tablespoon	70

Nuts

Almonds	8 nuts	100
Brazils	4 nuts	90
Walnuts	6 nuts	80
Chestnuts	4 nuts	30

Vegetables

An average helping of most vegetables only contains 20–25 calories (but don't forget to make allowances for any oil or butter used in cooking). Therefore, I've only listed vegetables with a high calorie content – again remember to allow for any butter you may add to them.

Beans:

baked	on 1 slice toast	180
broad, boiled	2 tablespoons	50
butter, boiled	2 tablespoons	80
haricot, boiled	2 tablespoons	80
Beetroot, boiled	4 slices	40
Corn, tinned	2 tablespoons	100
Lentils, boiled	2 tablespoons	80
Parsnips, boiled	3 tablespoons	50

Peas:

fresh, boiled	3 tablespoons	60
dried, boiled	3 tablespoons	120
tinned	3 tablespoons	100

Potatoes:

baked (in jacket)	1 medium	80
boiled	2 small	100
mashed	2 tablespoons	200
roast	2 small	140
fried	2 tablespoons	300

Cereals/Pasta

Rice, boiled	2 tablespoons	130
Breakfast cereals, average	6 tablespoons	100
Pasta	2 tablespoons	130
Porridge	3 tablespoons	80

Sugar/Sweets/Jams

Sugar, white/ brown	1 teaspoon	30
	1 tablespoon	110
Golden syrup	1 dessertspoon	80
Honey	1 dessertspoon	80
Jams/Marmalade	1 dessertspoon	70
Mincemeat	1 tablespoon	70

Sweets

Boiled sweets	2 sweets	45
chocolate: milk	1 small bar	250
plain	1 small bar	240
Toffees	2 toffees	60

Flour/Cakes/Biscuits

Flour	1 tablespoon	70
Bread: brown/ white, untoasted	1 medium slice	80
toasted	1 medium slice	80

Crispbread

Primula rye bread	1 slice	17
Ryvita	1 slice	29
Scanda Crisp	1 slice	19
Vitawheat	1 slice	32

Cakes

Currant buns	1 medium	150
Doughnuts	1 medium	250
Fruit cake	1 medium slice	300
Jam tarts	2 medium	300
Sponge cake	1 medium slice	180

Biscuits

Cream crackers	2 biscuits	70
Digestive	2 biscuits	130
Sweet	2 biscuits	120

BASIC GARDENING

The Basic Gardener's Calendar

(The information below is repeated in the relevant months of the diary to help you plan your gardening year.) However, as weather conditions vary so much between the north and south of the country, this has to be a general guide. Spring and summer usually arrive three or four weeks later in the north and Scotland, while winter comes in earlier – and lasts longer.

Rather unfairly, perhaps, most gardening guides, including this one, are based on southern conditions so you may need to adjust the timetable to suit your local climate. If you live in the north, this means that spring sowing and planting out should generally be delayed until late March or even early April. And you'll need to do all the pre-winter work outside a bit earlier to beat the frosts and freezes.

As it's extremely unlikely that you're measuring your garden with a metric tape, I've given Ancient British measurements, but for Eurogardeners basic measurement conversions are as follows:

3 inches – 7·5 cm	1 foot – 30 cm
6 inches – 15 cm	2 feet – 60 cm
9 inches – 22·5 cm	3 feet – 90 cm

January

Plan gardening year in front of fire. Decide on bulbs (indoor and out), grass (hopefully), vegetable patch (why not grow your own inexpensive vegetables?) and herbs in kitchen window box (to disguise mediocre food). Remember not to plant anything that will be at its best when *you* are on holiday.

February

Dig. Dig. Dig. Start a seed box or boxes in a warm kitchen, or buy a propagator: in case you don't know (I didn't), it's a sort of seed incubator and you can let plants grow in it until they're big enough to shove outside (this is called transplanting). Fill propagator with John Innes seed compost.

Sow cauliflower, sprouts, cabbage and leek seeds. Always sow greens in a seed bed or box and then transplant them to give them plenty of room to grow. *Language tip for beginners* – You sow a seed and you plant a plant. You can't sow a plant.

March

Many vegetable seeds can be sown out-doors from now on: start with broad beans, peas, parsnips. Plant leeks, shallots and onion sets (which are onions already partly grown).

New lawns can be sown.

Established lawns can enjoy a first mowing, if you must.

April

Sow more seeds out of doors, including peas, beetroot, turnips. Plant main crop potatoes.

Weed, weed, weed, to prevent weeds seeding.

May

Sow runner beans, building a cane bean frame for them to climb, or choose dwarf French beans, which need no support.

Sow seeds of winter cabbage and winter cauliflower in a cosy little corner of the garden, for transplanting later. Plant out the seedling cauliflowers, Brussels sprouts, cabbage and leeks you have raised in boxes or beds. If you don't want the trouble of raising them yourself, buy the young plants.

Keep the weeds down by hoeing.

Deal ruthlessly with slugs and snails as they do enormous damage to young plants.

June

Real growing things (peas and beans) start to appear.

Intense excitement!

Continue hoeing with added impetus.

Last chance to sow peas and beans from seed for second crop in September. Sow lettuce, chicory, radishes, turnips from seeds.

July

If you aren't on holiday, earth up potatoes ('earth up' means draw soil with a hoe around the potato stems).

Plant out winter cabbage and cauliflowers from seedbed.

Last chance to sow lettuce and radish seed.

August

Lift onions and shallots, dry in the sun (hopefully) and store. Sow cabbage in seedbed outside for next spring and early summer.

September

Lift potatoes when haulm (that's what the green part is called when it withers) is decayed. Allow to dry off for a few hours and store in the dark (or they go green and become poisonous).

October

Lift and store root crops, except parsnips, which you dig up as you need them. Plant out good specimens of August-sown cabbage.

Do not remove dead heads of hydrangeas; they form valuable protection for next year's buds.

November

Keep ground clean and young plants free from voracious, plundering slugs. Tidy up generally. Remove dead leaves from Brussels sprouts.

December

Back to the fire.

The Minimum Gardener

When to plant outdoor bulbs

Plant crocuses in September (3–4 inches deep, 2 inches apart)

Plant daffodils in Sept/Oct (4–6 inches deep, 6 inches apart)

Plant irises in Sept/Oct (3–4 inches deep, 6 inches apart)

Plant tulips in Oct/Nov (4–6 inches deep, 6 inches apart)

Plant snowdrops in Sept/Oct (3–4 inches deep, 6 inches apart)

Plant hyacinths in Sept/Nov (4–6 inches deep, 9 inches apart)

How to plant indoor bulbs (Crocuses, Daffodils, Tulips, Snowdrops, Hyacinths)

Plant in September/October, the larger the better, and buy special bulb fibre at the same time, because it will remain fresh throughout the growing season.

If you want Christmas flowering, buy bulbs marked 'pre-cooled' or 'prepared'. Plant immediately after purchasing. Place layer of fibre at bottom of pot (don't press down) then press bulb in the fibre, then add more fibre so that bulb tips just show above final fibre level. Put in a cool dark place at a temperature of about 55°F (but not in an airing cupboard; it's much too warm).

Keep fibre moist until young shoots show 2–3 inches (takes 8–12 weeks), then bring into normal temperature in shade. Keep damp.

Vegetable Sowing & Planting Guide

(If you're going to bother I suggest you concentrate on growing the more expensive vegetables)

Name	Sow or Plant	Distance Between Rows and Plants		When to Eat
Artichokes (Jerusalem)	(P) Feb–March	2½–3 ft	1 ft	Nov–March
Artichokes (Globe)	(P) April	2½–3 ft	2 ft	July–Sept
Asparagus	(P) April	1–1½ ft	1 ft	May–June
Beans				
broad	(S) Nov or (S) Feb–March	2 ft	6 in	June–Aug
French	(S) April–May	2 ft	9 in	July–Aug
runner	(S) May–June/(P) May	4–6 ft	9 in	July–Oct
Beetroot	(S) April–June	1 ft	4–6 in	All year
Brussels sprouts	(S) March/(P) May	2½ ft	2 ft	Nov–March
Broccoli (sprouting)	(S) April–May/(P) June–July	2 ft	2 ft	Feb–May
Cabbage				
spring	(S) Aug/(P) Sept	1½ ft	1½ ft	March–May
summer	(S) April/(P) May	2 ft	2 ft	June–Aug
autumn	(S) April–May/(P) June	2 ft	2 ft	Sept–Oct
winter	(S) May/(P) July	2 ft	2 ft	Nov–Jan
Carrots				
early	(S) March–April	1 ft	3 in	June–Aug
main	(S) May	1 ft	6 in	Sept–May
Cauliflower				
summer	(S) March–April/(P) April–June	2 ft	2 ft	July–Sept
autumn	(S) April–May/(P) June	2 ft	2 ft	Oct–May
winter	(S) April–May/(P) July	2 ft	2 ft	Dec–May
Leeks	(S) March/(P) May–June	1 ft	9 in	Nov–March
Lettuce				
summer	(S) March–July/(P) April–May	1 ft	9 in	May–Oct
winter	(S) Aug–Sept/(P) Oct	1 ft	6 in	April–May
Marrows	(S) May/(P) May–June	3–4 ft	3–4 ft	July–Nov
Onion	(S) March or Aug/(P) April	1 ft	6 in	All year
Onion (sets)	(P) March	1 ft	6 in	Aug–April
Parsnip	(S) Feb–March	1–1½ ft	6–9 in	Nov–March
Potatoes				
early	(P) March	2 ft	12–15 in	June–Oct
main	(P) April–May	2½ ft	15 in	Oct–May
Radishes	(S) March–Sept	1 ft	1–2 in	April–Sept
Rhubarb	(P) March	3 ft	3 ft	April–Aug
Swedes	(S) June	1 ft	9 in	Oct–March
Tomatoes	(P) March–June	2 ft	1½ ft	Aug–Oct
Turnips	(S) March–June	1 ft	9 in	June–Nov

Bottling Chart

FRUIT	Jan	Feb	Mar	Apr	May	June	July	Aug	Sept	Oct	Nov	Dec
Apples									●	●	●	
Apricots							●	●				
Bilberries							●	●				
Blackberries								●	●	●		
Blackcurrants						●	●					
Damsons								●	●			
Gooseberries						●	●					
Greengages								●	●			
Loganberries							●	●				
Peaches								●	●	●		
Pears									●	◐		
Plums							●	●				
Quinces								●	●			
Raspberries						●	●					
Redcurrants					●	●						
Rhubarb				●	●							
Strawberries				●	●							
Whitecurrants					●	●						

When to grow herbs

Name	When	Distance Apart	Use for
Basil	April–May	1 ft	Dry for winter. Soup, sauce
Borage	April–May	1 ft	Beverages
Chervil	March–June Sow every 6 weeks	1 ft	Salads, soup
Chives	Divide March or April	6 in	Cut often. Salad, soup
Fennel	April–May	1½ ft	Salad, fish
Garlic	March (2 inches down)	9 in	Harvest in August. Store
Horseradish	Set root cuttings in March in raised beds 2 ft high	1 ft	Sauce
Marjoram	Sow March–April	9 in	Stew, soup. Dry for winter
Mint	Divide roots Oct or March. Renew every 3 years	1 ft	Sauce, vegetables
Parsley	Sow April and July. Slow to germinate	6 in	Sauce, garnish
Rosemary	May	2 ft	Evergreen. Lamb, fruit salads, drinks
Sage	April–May	2 ft	Stuffing. Dry for winter
Thyme	April–May	9 in	Stuffing. Dry for winter

CALENDARS FOR 1976-1977-1978

Calendar 1976

January

S	M	T	W	T	F	S
.	.	.	.	1	2	3
4	5	6	7	8	9	10
11	12	13	14	15	16	17
18	19	20	21	22	23	24
25	26	27	28	29	30	31

February

S	M	T	W	T	F	S
1	2	3	4	5	6	7
8	9	10	11	12	13	14
15	16	17	18	19	20	21
22	23	24	25	26	27	28
29	.	.	.	.	.	.

March

S	M	T	W	T	F	S
.	1	2	3	4	5	6
7	8	9	10	11	12	13
14	15	16	17	18	19	20
21	22	23	24	25	26	27
28	29	30	31	.	.	.

April

S	M	T	W	T	F	S
.	.	.	.	1	2	3
4	5	6	7	8	9	10
11	12	13	14	15	16	17
18	19	20	21	22	23	24
25	26	27	28	29	30	.

May

S	M	T	W	T	F	S
.	.	.	.	.	.	1
2	3	4	5	6	7	8
9	10	11	12	13	14	15
16	17	18	19	20	21	22
23	24	25	26	27	28	29
30	31	.	.	.	.	.

June

S	M	T	W	T	F	S
.	.	1	2	3	4	5
6	7	8	9	10	11	12
13	14	15	16	17	18	19
20	21	22	23	24	25	26
27	28	29	30	.	.	.

July

S	M	T	W	T	F	S
.	.	.	.	1	2	3
4	5	6	7	8	9	10
11	12	13	14	15	16	17
18	19	20	21	22	23	24
25	26	27	28	29	30	31

August

S	M	T	W	T	F	S
1	2	3	4	5	6	7
8	9	10	11	12	13	14
15	16	17	18	19	20	21
22	23	24	25	26	27	28
29	30	31	.	.	.	.

September

S	M	T	W	T	F	S
.	.	.	1	2	3	4
5	6	7	8	9	10	11
12	13	14	15	16	17	18
19	20	21	22	23	24	25
26	27	28	29	30	.	.

October

S	M	T	W	T	F	S
.	.	.	.	.	1	2
3	4	5	6	7	8	9
10	11	12	13	14	15	16
17	18	19	20	21	22	23
24	25	26	27	28	29	30
31	.	.	.	.	.	.

November

S	M	T	W	T	F	S
.	1	2	3	4	5	6
7	8	9	10	11	12	13
14	15	16	17	18	19	20
21	22	23	24	25	26	27
28	29	30	.	.	.	.

December

S	M	T	W	T	F	S
.	.	.	1	2	3	4
5	6	7	8	9	10	11
12	13	14	15	16	17	18
19	20	21	22	23	24	25
26	27	28	29	30	31	.

Calendar 1977

January

S	M	T	W	T	F	S
.	.	.	.	.	.	1
2	3	4	5	6	7	8
9	10	11	12	13	14	15
16	17	18	19	20	21	22
23	24	25	26	27	28	29
30	31	.	.	.	.	.

February

S	M	T	W	T	F	S
.	.	1	2	3	4	5
6	7	8	9	10	11	12
13	14	15	16	17	18	19
20	21	22	23	24	25	26
27	28	.	.	.	.	.

March

S	M	T	W	T	F	S
.	.	1	2	3	4	5
6	7	8	9	10	11	12
13	14	15	16	17	18	19
20	21	22	23	24	25	26
27	28	29	30	31	.	.

April

S	M	T	W	T	F	S
.	.	.	.	.	1	2
3	4	5	6	7	8	9
10	11	12	13	14	15	16
17	18	19	20	21	22	23
24	25	26	27	28	29	30

May

S	M	T	W	T	F	S
1	2	3	4	5	6	7
8	9	10	11	12	13	14
15	16	17	18	19	20	21
22	23	24	25	26	27	28
29	30	31	.	.	.	.

June

S	M	T	W	T	F	S
.	.	.	1	2	3	4
5	6	7	8	9	10	11
12	13	14	15	16	17	18
19	20	21	22	23	24	25
26	27	28	29	30	.	.

July

S	M	T	W	T	F	S
.	.	.	.	.	1	2
3	4	5	6	7	8	9
10	11	12	13	14	15	16
17	18	19	20	21	22	23
24	25	26	27	28	29	30
31	.	.	.	.	.	.

August

S	M	T	W	T	F	S
.	1	2	3	4	5	6
7	8	9	10	11	12	13
14	15	16	17	18	19	20
21	22	23	24	25	26	27
28	29	30	31	.	.	.

September

S	M	T	W	T	F	S
.	.	.	.	1	2	3
4	5	6	7	8	9	10
11	12	13	14	15	16	17
18	19	20	21	22	23	24
25	26	27	28	29	30	.

October

S	M	T	W	T	F	S
.	.	.	.	.	.	1
2	3	4	5	6	7	8
9	10	11	12	13	14	15
16	17	18	19	20	21	22
23	24	25	26	27	28	29
30	31	.	.	.	.	.

November

S	M	T	W	T	F	S
.	.	1	2	3	4	5
6	7	8	9	10	11	12
13	14	15	16	17	18	19
20	21	22	23	24	25	26
27	28	29	30	.	.	.

December

S	M	T	W	T	F	S
.	.	.	.	1	2	3
4	5	6	7	8	9	10
11	12	13	14	15	16	17
18	19	20	21	22	23	24
25	26	27	28	29	30	31

Calendar 1978

January

S	M	T	W	T	F	S
1	2	3	4	5	6	7
8	9	10	11	12	13	14
15	16	17	18	19	20	21
22	23	24	25	26	27	28
29	30	31	.	.	.	.

February

S	M	T	W	T	F	S
.	.	.	1	2	3	4
5	6	7	8	9	10	11
12	13	14	15	16	17	18
19	20	21	22	23	24	25
26	27	28	.	.	.	.

March

S	M	T	W	T	F	S
.	.	.	1	2	3	4
5	6	7	8	9	10	11
12	13	14	15	16	17	18
19	20	21	22	23	24	25
26	27	28	29	30	31	.

April

S	M	T	W	T	F	S
.	.	.	.	.	.	1
2	3	4	5	6	7	8
9	10	11	12	13	14	15
16	17	18	19	20	21	22
23	24	25	26	27	28	29
30	.	.	.	.	.	.

May

S	M	T	W	T	F	S
.	1	2	3	4	5	6
7	8	9	10	11	12	13
14	15	16	17	18	19	20
21	22	23	24	25	26	27
28	29	30	31	.	.	.

June

S	M	T	W	T	F	S
.	.	.	.	1	2	3
4	5	6	7	8	9	10
11	12	13	14	15	16	17
18	19	20	21	22	23	24
25	26	27	28	29	30	.

July

S	M	T	W	T	F	S
.	.	.	.	.	.	1
2	3	4	5	6	7	8
9	10	11	12	13	14	15
16	17	18	19	20	21	22
23	24	25	26	27	28	29
30	31	.	.	.	.	.

August

S	M	T	W	T	F	S
.	.	1	2	3	4	5
6	7	8	9	10	11	12
13	14	15	16	17	18	19
20	21	22	23	24	25	26
27	28	29	30	31	.	.

September

S	M	T	W	T	F	S
.	.	.	.	.	1	2
3	4	5	6	7	8	9
10	11	12	13	14	15	16
17	18	19	20	21	22	23
24	25	26	27	28	29	30

October

S	M	T	W	T	F	S
1	2	3	4	5	6	7
8	9	10	11	12	13	14
15	16	17	18	19	20	21
22	23	24	25	26	27	28
29	30	31	.	.	.	.

November

S	M	T	W	T	F	S
.	.	.	1	2	3	4
5	6	7	8	9	10	11
12	13	14	15	16	17	18
19	20	21	22	23	24	25
26	27	28	29	30	.	.

December

S	M	T	W	T	F	S
.	.	.	.	.	1	2
3	4	5	6	7	8	9
10	11	12	13	14	15	16
17	18	19	20	21	22	23
24	25	26	27	28	29	30
31	.	.	.	.	.	.

WHERE THE MONEY OUGHT TO GO...

It's just as well to decide in advance roughly how you intend to split up your spending money. However, if it doesn't work (highly likely) it's just as well to notice, say, that you're spending in July twice the amount on meat that you thought you would in January. Seeing at the beginning of the year what my annual budget sum is for an item like, say, dry cleaning, makes me gasp at the yearly total, and then I start being mean about dry cleaning right from the first week of January.

I think that on the whole it's unrealistic for anyone to tell anyone else what percentages of their income they should be spending on rent, savings, showgirls or gin. Everybody has different needs, wants and priorities. However, my spending list will probably include some of the following: rent/mortage repayment, rates, taxes, insurance, household expenses (including food, fuel, laundry, telephone), clothes, holidays, savings and insurance, subscriptions . . .

List them for yourself, put down the yearly sum allowed and then the weekly or monthly sum, whichever way you organize your finances. And good luck to you.

WHERE THE MONEY WENT

Items (You fill in this column – rent, mortgage, etc.)	January £ P	February £ P	March £ P	April £ P	May £ P	June £ P

Grand sum spent for half year £   P

July		August		September		October		November		December		Yearly Total	
£	p	£	p	£	p	£	p	£	p	£	p	£	p

Grand sum spent this year £   p

January

ARIES

In the beginning, God made Aries people and in so doing created a lot of problems for the other eleven signs of the Zodiac. All that energy, vitality, drive and determination! But is it true that Arians are by nature headstrong, impulsive, impetuous and impatient? Yes. Perhaps your New Year resolution should be 'In 1977 I will make a concerted effort to think before I act.' You had better think long and hard about your work and career prospects this January. The Sun, together with your own ruling planet Mars, will be passing through the midheaven point of your solar horoscope, which means the boss will be unusually tetchy, exacting and unsympathetic. However, the financial outlook is encouraging this month, and favourable trends continue until early April.

TAURUS

The year opens with Jupiter in Taurus, where it will remain until April 3, so in a way during the first three months of 1977 you are afforded some kind of protection; but with the unpredictable planet Uranus in your angle of matrimonial and partnership affairs, and the dour Saturn in your area of home and family concerns, you are going to need it! Because Taurus is an Earth sign and your planetary ruler is Venus, you desire and frequently acquire the good things in life. Now it looks as if you are being forced to unload rather than collect any more possessions and encumbrances. In fact, over the next couple of years with Saturn in Leo you will begin to realize the truth in the adage that there are no pockets in shrouds.

GEMINI

Astrological tradition tells us that people born under the sign of Gemini live mostly in the mind, that you are usually refined, mentally versatile, fond of change and variety, highly strung and much affected by those with whom you come in contact. What it doesn't tell us is that you are frequently suspicious of your own feelings, over-sensitive, and at times not easy to live with. However, it won't be in the area of your emotions that you are confused this January, but in relation to things of a financial or business nature. Your ruling planet Mercury is in what is called retrograde motion, meaning that it appears to be travelling backwards through the heavens, between the 1st and 18th, and you would be very unwise indeed to give or extract promises – you could be conned.

CANCER

Water signs, of which Cancer is the first, always look upon the world as something against which they must defend themselves, and this is particularly noticeable with the Crab, which develops a hard outer shell to protect its inner sensitiveness. The Sun is passing through your opposite sign of Capricorn between January 1 and 20 making you even more vulnerable and unable to gauge how either partners or loved ones will act or react. If you anticipate them being changeable, moody and argumentative you won't be far wrong. Since Saturn moved out of your own birthsign in early June last year, you have probably been very much preoccupied with matters related to income and financial security, and the current planetary picture suggests you are far from being out of the wood yet.

LEO

There is nothing petty, secretive or underhand about Leos. Your emotions are dominant, positive and outgoing. Unfortunately, with the baleful planet Saturn now passing through your own birthsign you are being forced to re-evaluate and retrench. However, Saturn has been in Leo since last June and will remain a kind of restraining factor until the middle of 1978, so the sooner you begin to accept the demands and limitations it imposes, the more patient and practical you will become. Career and professional changes are very much on the cards this January. Do, however, wait until after the 18th before handing in your notice or accepting new appointments. After the Sun enters your opposite sign of Aquarius on the 21st, circumstances will force you to devote more time to matrimonial interests.

VIRGO

Each year while the Sun is in Capricorn until January 20, you are supposed to be having a lovely time because this is when others are more likely to tell you that you are attractive, intelligent and a lot of fun, and you can only blame your own ruling planet Mercury, which is retrograde until the 18th, if, instead, you are charged with being critical, unimaginative, over-ambitious and too preoccupied with feathering your own nest. Undoubtedly you will have the last word on the subject and flay your detractors, but you may as well expect January to be a turbulent month emotionally. Battle if you must, but you should know by now that when your nervous forces are depleted by the mental strain to which you subject yourself, there are always tears before bed-time.

LIBRA

What is this myth that all Librans are well-balanced, kind and affable? Affectionate, sociable and pleasure-loving, certainly; well-balanced – never! It's the search for the balance and the inability to strike it which makes you so impulsively generous, changeable and over-dependent on others. The year opens with the Sun, Mercury and Mars all together in your angle of home and domestic affairs, and if you haven't found permanent solutions to this kind of problem in 1976, then you must now begin to prove just how resolute, adamant and bloody-minded you can be. 1977 should be a year of immense career opportunities for you, but here again you must be prepared to go it alone. You probably think you are at your best when collaborating with others, but, don't you always contribute more than your share?

SCORPIO

The quickest way to empty a room is not by screaming fire – but Scorpio! To be involved with one can be likened to having a ringside seat at the summit of Mount Etna. And now, with the dynamic planet Uranus firmly esconced in your own birthsign, anyone with half a mind will have sensed that somehow, somewhere, you are about to take off. 1976 was probably a peculiar year for matrimonial and partnership affairs - perhaps 'decisive' would be more accurate – and it won't be until April that this frustrating chapter comes to a close; only then will you realize where you are going, who is, and more important still, who is definitely not going with you. Someone once declared that martyr-dom is, of course, Scorpionic.

SAGITTARIUS

Your opposite sign in the Zodiac is Gemini, and the only person who would really understand and appreciate your current financial difficulties would be either a Geminian or another Sagittarian; because the Sun, Mercury and Mars in Capricorn this January accentuate partnership money problems for them and personal ones for you. Your own ruling planet Jupiter remains in Taurus until the beginning of April; during the next three months you ought to try and reappraise work and career prospects, and if necessary consider making a major move or change. There are no adverse planetary aspects this month relating to either partnerships or emotional relationships so at least you won't have that kind of problem.

CAPRICORN

You may not have to be told that your own ruling planet Saturn is now in your angle of joint finances and business affairs – the bills and overdrafts will speak for themselves – but Saturn is not only the great leveller and taskmaster of the Zodiac, it is also the great reaper, so those who have sown little will now have little to reap. But for all of you January is going to be a challenging month, because not only the Sun, but also Mars, and Mercury in retrograde motion are all operating in your own birthsign. What this really means is you have probably pushed yourself too hard and the planets are telling you it's time to let up and unwind. There are principally two types of Capricorn, the active and expressive, and the reserved, quiet and plodding, but ambition is the common denominator.

AQUARIUS

Prior to the discovery of Uranus in 1781 by Herschel, Saturn was thought to be the ruler of Aquarius, and in some ways it still can be associated with the darker and more introspective side of your character; now, because it is currently passing through your opposite sign of Leo, you are bound to learn just how tough and demanding Saturn can be. More than ever before, you must strive to keep partnerships and close relationships intact; that is, of course, if you really do want to remain attached. The month before one's own birthday is invariably a bit dreary, so until January 21 you are going to be very much on your own and somewhat introspective. A time to reassess and reappraise situations rather than force very personal issues out into the open.

PISCES

Why is it that Pisces is always considered to be the poor relation of the Zodiac, when in fact you are probably more imaginative, inventive and creative than all the other eleven signs put together? Certainly, no one is more emotional than you; you have all the generosity and restlessness of Jupiter, and all the elusiveness of Neptune. Impressionable and adaptable, you possess the chameleon-like quality of taking on the nature of your surroundings and of the people you meet. Pisces are born actors – so pull out all the stops and give your best performance this January, and some kind of acceptance or recognition is assured. Friends, however, will not be easily impressed – in fact, one relationship seems to be past repair.

JANUARY

Monday

Tuesday

Wednesday

Thursday

Friday

Saturday
1

New Year's Day. Public holiday.
Camping, Outdoor Life, Travel and Motor Caravan
Exhibition at Olympia, London (to January 9).

Sunday
2

Ignore the weather. Think summer holidays. Get travel
brochures. Fill blank lists in diary.

Supertip
Ignore the weather. Think
summer holidays. Get travel
brochures. Fill blank lists in
diary.

Supertip
Hangovers are dehydrating. If
you're suffering, drink anything
except what you drank. Try
quaffing soda water, Coca-cola
or cold milk.

Some winter sales start today.
No impulse buys. Go out with
a list of what you want and
buy nothing else. Remember
all the things you have bought
at sales and never worn.
What you need to buy are
things that are not fun but
cheaper in the sales. Head for
linen and household
departments; china, glass,
cutlery, kitchen equipment,
saucepans, pressure cooker and
(oddly enough) shoes.

Supertip
Feathered game is nearing end of
season. Wily old birds which
have escaped guns now
inexpensive and make excellent
casseroles and pâtés to freeze for
later use.

Reputation Maker

Nerve Juice

A pick-me-up. Good for hangovers or when you haven't time for breakfast or lunch. Makes half a pint (3 dl).

Ingredients
juice of 1 orange
1 raw egg
1 large teaspoon runny honey

Method
1 Put all ingredients in a blender or blend with beater until well mixed.
2 Serve in a wineglass with crushed ice.

Gardening

January Gardener

Plan gardening year in front of fire. Decide on bulbs (indoor and out), grass (hopefully), vegetable patch (why not grow your own inexpensive vegetables?) and herbs in kitchen window box (to disguise mediocre food). Remember not to plant anything that will be at its best when *you* are on holiday.

Traditional Dish

Toad-in-the-hole
Ingredients
4 oz/100 g plain flour
2 eggs
½ pint/3 dl milk
1–1½ lb/450–675 g sausages
½ lb/225 g bacon with rinds removed and rashers cut in half
salt and pepper

Method
1 Make batter, by sieving flour and seasoning into a large bowl.
2 Make a well in centre of flour, add eggs and beat until well mixed.
3 Gradually stir in half the milk, beating well and ensuring there are no lumps.
4 Add remaining milk and beat for another 5–8 minutes.
5 Heat empty, well-greased baking dish in oven at Mark 7/425°F/220°C.
6 Wrap each sausage in bacon rasher.
7 Arrange sausages in hot baking dish.
8 Pour batter over sausages and bake for 35–40 minutes.

JANUARY

Monday
 3

Bank Holiday, Scotland.

Motherlore
A mother's place is in the wrong.

Tuesday
 4

Get children's school things ready for spring term.

Wednesday
 5

Blissful thought: Children start school soon.
Boat Show opens at Earls Court, London (to January 15).

Motherlore
Why do people only tell you to pull yourself together when you can't?

Thursday
 6

Feast of the Epiphany (commemorates the Three Kings arriving to see the baby Jesus at Bethlehem).
Twelfth Night – throw out tree. Pack away decorations.

Friday
 7

Don't give up your evening classes. Remember why you joined. Remember you may not be able to join any other evening classes until next September.

Rethink New Year Resolutions. Undecide to give up food and drink. Try some simpler resolve, such as washing up milk saucepan immediately after use.

Saturday
 8

Up on that roof! Final gutter check for last of autumn leaves.

Supertip
Resolve next year to put sheet or towel under tree and shake corners to middle every morning, thus avoiding sharp pine needles throughout happy home.

Sunday
9

Time to:
Check insurance/car licence/TV licence/membership renewals/passport/car and household equipment servicing/roof, gutters, chimneys/transfer items from old diary to new diary including family birthdays.

Family Favourite

Computer Winter Salad

To a salad bowl of grated white cabbage or sliced chicory add two of the following:

Ingredients
1 peeled orange, thinly sliced in rounds
1 peeled apple, thinly sliced in rounds
1 finely sliced small leek
1 chopped green pepper
6 chopped radishes
a few finely cut slices of raw turnip
a handful of cold cooked runner beans
 (or possibly leftover frozen beans)

Method
Mix with French dressing and serve with one of the following sprinkled over the salad:
1 dessertspoon currants
1 teaspoon caraway seeds
1 dessertspoon capers
4 chopped anchovies

Gardening

The Non-gardener's Incentive to Start a Vegetable Patch

Fact 1. An area 10 yards long by 10 yards wide is big enough to provide a family of four with carrots, turnips and runner beans in summer; cabbages, leeks and sprouts in winter.

Fact 2. You can expect 36 lb/16 kg of main crop potatoes from every 10-yard trench cultivated.

Reputation Maker

Willow's Smoked Salmon

Remove skin and bones from a raw kipper with a sharp knife. Marinate in French dressing for two hours. Slice thinly and serve with lots of pepper and wedges of lemon.

To make 'smoked salmon' sandwiches, do not marinate in vinaigrette but slice thinly, put on a slice of thinly cut crustless brown bread, add pepper and lemon juice, roll up and serve.

JANUARY

Monday
10

Spanish Seville oranges now in the shops ready for marmalade making.

Tuesday
11

Wednesday
12

Thursday
13

Friday
14

Saturday
15

Two big Rugby Union International Matches today:
Wales *v* Ireland at Cardiff;
England *v* Scotland at Twickenham.

Sunday
16

Supertip
To make your own self-cleaning oven, start with a clean oven, then make sure you never have to do the job again.
Here's how: Mix 1 tablespoon bicarbonate of soda with half a pint (3 dl) of warm water. Wring out clean cloth with this solution and wipe over inside of oven, including roasting pan and shelves. When dry there's a slightly chalky powder left but I'm prepared to put up with that for a quick, cheap, easy oven-cleaner. On no account use this method on an oven with a special self-cleaning lining.

Motherlore
Why not continue to make life easier for everyone around you by making life easier for yourself? How? Cultivate the power of negative thinking. PLAN. Aim to do less and achieve more.

Supertip
To get a burnt saucepan clean, fill with warm water in which you dissolve half a cup of biological detergent. Soak overnight. You may need to do it several nights, depending how dreadful the saucepan is.

Motherlore
Before you buy, ask 'Do I want it, or do I NEED it?'

Traditional Dish

Traditional Scottish Chunky Marmalade

Makes about 5 lb/2¼ kg. Takes 2 hours and can be a messy business (wrap up well) but really worth the effort and a pot makes a good present.

Ingredients

1½ lb/675 g Seville oranges, with navel removed
juice of 1 lemon
3 pints/1.8 litres water
3 lb/1¼ kg brown or white sugar★
½ oz/15 g butter

Method

1 Scrub oranges and put them whole in a large saucepan.
2 Add water, bring to boil, then reduce heat, cover pan and simmer gently for 1½–2 hours (or until orange skin is soft).
3 Remove oranges from pan, cool slightly, cut in half and remove pips. Tie pips in a muslin bag (or handkerchief). Chop orange into matchstick thin strips.
4 Return chopped oranges to pan with lemon juice and bag of pips. (It's very important to cook the pips – a source of pectin.)
5 Add sugar, heat slowly, stirring all the time with a wooden spoon, until sugar has dissolved.
6 Bring to boil and boil steadily until setting point is reached (at least 40 minutes). To test, put a small spoonful of marmalade on a small plate, chill as fast as possible, then push jam gently with forefinger. If it crinkles and a drop of jam on your finger will not fall, your marmalade will set. Remove pan from heat while giving this test, or it may overcook.
7 Remove pan from heat and stir in butter.
8 Leave marmalade in pan until a skin forms on top.
9 Stir gently, pour into pots standing on newspaper. Cover pots.

Notes

If you have a blender, pulverize the lemon peel and add it with the lemon juice (see step 4 above).
★ Use white sugar for an orange-coloured marmalade, brown for a rich dark preserve.

If you like a sweet marmalade add 1½ lb/675 g more sugar.
If you have a tablespoon of rum around, after step 8 put a small pudding basinful of marmalade aside, stir in the rum and you have a Jamaican marmalade.

JANUARY

Monday
17

Tuesday
18

Wednesday
19

Thursday
20

Friday
21

Saturday
22

Sunday
23

Supertip
A bag in a sink tidy makes emptying it easier.

Supertip
When washing venetian blinds, wear woolly socks on your hands so they don't get scratched or torn.

Supertip
A fresh pepper, whether red or green, lasts about three weeks and tastes delicious shredded into salad. And however shrivelled, when chopped into almost any stew dish it imparts an inimitable Continental flavour.

Motherlore
Emergencies always happen when they're late for school. Have a box ready with:
1 A needle threaded with white and a needle threaded with black cotton both doubled and knotted.
2 Shoelaces
3 Buttons
4 Loose coins for fares, if necessary
5 Safety pins

Family Favourite

Cauliflower Au Gratin

Ingredients

1 cauliflower
1½ oz/40 g butter
1 oz/25 g flour
4 oz/100 g grated cheese
½ pint/3 dl milk
salt and pepper

Method

1 Remove coarse outer leaves, cut a cross in the stalk and wash cauliflower.
2 Cook (stem side down) in boiling, salted water until softer (but not sloppy) and put in ovenproof dish.
3 In a separate saucepan, melt butter, stir in flour and cook on low heat for a few minutes.
4 Remove pan from heat and gradually add milk, stirring all the time.
5 Return to heat and continue to stir until sauce thickens.
6 Add most of cheese and season to taste.
7 Pour sauce over cauliflower and sprinkle top with remaining cheese.
8 Brown under a hot grill and serve piping hot.

Family Favourite

French Onion Tart

Ingredients

6 oz/175 g shortcrust pastry
1½–2 lb/675–900 g onions, peeled and finely sliced
2 beaten eggs
2 oz/50 g Gruyère cheese, or mild Cheddar, grated
salt and pepper

Method

1 Roll out pastry and line an 8-inch (21-cm) round flan ring. Trim edges, prick base well and bake at Mark 4/350°F/180°C for 10 minutes.
2 Cook onions gently in butter, until transparent, keeping the pan covered.
3 Remove from heat and stir in eggs and cheese. Season well.
4 Turn mixture into pastry case and bake at Mark 4/350°F/180°C for 35–40 minutes.

JANUARY

Monday
24

Tuesday
25

Wednesday
26

Australia Day.
Paul Newman's birthday. He is 52 (born 1925).

Thursday
27

Friday
28

Saturday
29

Sunday
30

Snowdrops are coming out – the first flowers of spring.
Leave them where they are.

Supertip
Get felt pen stains off shirts with soap and warm water. Remove ballpoint pen stains with methylated spirits.

Supertip
Remove egg stains from silver spoons by rubbing them with lemon juice and fine salt. If stains are old, soak spoons in very hot soapy water with added eggcup of ammonia.

Motherlore
Start asking yourself why not?

Supertip
To remove white rings on wood, remove build-up of polish with cloth dipped in methylated spirit. If necessary, gently rub down surface with finest wire wool. Recolour with Topps Scratch Polish or boot polish or half a walnut or a brazil nut. Then repolish.

Winter Warmer

Braised Pig's Liver
Ingredients
1 whole pig's liver (about 2 lb/900 g)
16 rashers of bacon
6 peeled carrots
1 onion, peeled and stuck with a clove
1 bayleaf
1 pinch thyme
1 handful parsley
peppercorns
clove of garlic, crushed
1 cup white wine
1 pint/6 dl stock (or water)
salt

Method
1 Keep the liver in one piece and with a sharp, pointed knife make a row of small incisions.
2 Roll small pieces of bacon in pepper and place into each incision.
3 Line the bottom of a casserole with 4 rashers of bacon and place the liver on top.
4 Pour over enough white wine and stock or water (in equal quantities) to just cover the liver.
5 Add carrots, onion, bayleaf, thyme, parsley, a few peppercorns and the garlic. Season to taste.
6 Put another 8 rashers of bacon over the liver.
7 Cover the casserole and cook gently in oven at Mark 3/325°F/160°C for about 30 minutes, until the liver is just tender.
8 Strain off sauce, removing any excess fat; put sauce into a small pan and reduce by half.
9 When the sauce is thick enough, add a knob of butter and pour over the liver.
10 Serve immediately, with rice, noodles or mashed potatoes.

Reputation Maker

Prawns Provençale
Ingredients
1 lb/450 g prawns
2 cloves garlic, peeled and crushed
¼ lb/100 g butter
handful chopped parsley
salt and pepper

Method
1 Mash garlic into butter, then add parsley.
2 Shell prawns (except a few to garnish), season and put either into individual cocotte dishes or one fireproof dish.
3 Cover with parsley butter and leave – but do not cook – in a very hot, turned-off oven for 10 minutes before serving.

February

ARIES

February is a funny month, because until the 18th the Sun and various planets in Aquarius relate well to Pluto in your angle of matrimonial and partnership affairs, but unfortunately they oppose Saturn in Leo. This indicates some kind of emotional crisis, which has probably been steadily brewing away since June 1976, and you must now decide where your love and loyalties lie. The Ram has always been a sacrificial animal in ancient literature, and Aries is the adolescent who has just realized the pulsating life-force within and yet is often very shy and timid when confronted by the need to display that newfound energy. We invariably get to know how to make a success of something after we have seen how it should not be done, and those who are never mistaken will probably never discover much.

TAURUS

Whereas Arians scatter their forces, Taurians conserve them, and you are always considered to be cautious, stubborn, plodding, practical and sometimes bordering on boring. February's aspects afford you an opportunity to prove just how ambitious, enterprising and outspoken you can be when you decide the time has come to seek promotion or recognition at work. The Sun in Aquarius until the 18th should ensure that people in a position of strength or authority will give you a sympathetic hearing, but unfortunately the same cannot be said about relatives and loved ones. Saturn in Leo opposed by the Sun, Mars and Mercury presents a gloomy picture. Bend over backwards to please and placate rather than become obstinate and recalcitrant.

GEMINI

The most obvious interpretation of the symbol for Gemini is the roman numeral two, II. This defines perfectly the dualistic nature of the sign. But people born with the Sun in Gemini are many-sided and it now looks as if you are being forced to accept once and for all who you are, what you are and where you're going. With the Sun and a plethora of planets in your angle of long-distance travel this February you could well be making plans which will take you away from your usual environment in the very near future. First you must cope with a series of oppositions to Saturn. The basic Gemini character is essentially that of the child who continually asks 'why?', and with Saturn in Leo for the next couple of years you are going to find out why personal relationships have failed in the past.

CANCER

There's no point in beating about the bush, February will probably be the most difficult month of the year for both personal and partnership finances; also business and legal matters. In fact, it's likely to be crunch time and it will take all your Cancerian tenacity and resourcefulness to get you through unscathed. One of your big problems is that you can't let go and you tend to dwell far too much in the past. If you really know that something isn't working now, cut your losses and get out. After a couple of excruciating years personally and emotionally you now find you have to devote so much time and energy to protecting your material interests and future security. However, this is one occasion when you really just cannot afford to play the martyr.

LEO

If it is true that Leos like things laid on the line and appreciate the unvarnished truth, then read on. Your solar horoscope looks like a battlefield, and it is unlikely that you will be the victor in any matrimonial or partnership conflicts. The Sun, Mars and Mercury all oppose Saturn in Leo, so you are bound to be unusually vulnerable, introspective and at times despondent. However, the lovely thing about astrology is that the planets are always on the move, and once you have learned the lesson adverse aspects are intent on teaching you, you emerge stronger, wiser, and hopefully more tolerant. 'The starting point of love is the sacrifice of that which in us opposes all sacrifice' – Vinet.

VIRGO

Saturn is currently passing through Leo, where it stresses twelfth house matters. Just as there are twelve signs of the Zodiac, there are also twelve houses of a horoscope, each one representing a specific area of one's life. For instance, the first is the Ego and outward character, the second income and personal finances, and so on. The twelfth relates to one's very private thoughts, secrets, and what one prefers to conceal from the world. Now it appears you must come out of your shell, face up to reality and tackle both emotional and career problems rather than give others the wrong impression. You may not have your usual amount of stamina this February but you will become progressively stronger by refusing to capitulate.

LIBRA

Libra is an Air sign, and people born under its influence must be constantly circulating. Your realm is people and parties. However, you must now decide who you really do care about. There are bound to be some people you would prefer never to see again. Old people are definitely going to be a big problem this month, but if you are a typical Libran you find it virtually impossible to upset anyone. However, don't indulge in your propensity to let things slide. Difficulties evaded continually return although in another form, and if you are to capitalize on your artistic and creative talents then you must be free. Ask yourself this question – who is it that spends most sleepless nights worrying about finances and the future? – not partners, loved ones and friends, but you, so learn to say no.

SCORPIO

Each February until around the 18th, while the Sun is in Aquarius, your attention is directed towards developments which in some way relate to your home life or domestic situation. This month is no exception and unfortunately a series of adverse planetary aspects indicates that some kind of a showdown is inevitable. Maybe you believe that any change would be a change for the better, but with Saturn currently passing through the midheaven of your solar horoscope a break or separation would be an expensive business both emotionally and financially. You have, as you know, a remarkable faculty for detecting the weak points in the characters of others, but this is one month when it is your defects and deficiencies that could prove an embarrassment.

SAGITTARIUS

Sagittarians have much in common with Aries folk. You are both restless, impulsive and occasionally too frank and direct in your approach. Sagittarius, as you know, is the Archer, shooting his arrow straight to its mark. Ruled by Jupiter, you are supposed to be born lucky, but the way you sometimes carry on and complain, especially to the rest of the family, one would think you were never appreciated, understood or thanked for your efforts. It will take an incredible amount of effort on your part this February to keep the peace with relatives, close associates and colleagues. Your every word and move will be noted and recorded, so while showing them that you have ability and a sense of purpose prove also that you have not lost your sense of fun, or, better still, your sense of the ridiculous.

CAPRICORN

It is your own ruling planet Saturn in Leo opposed by the Sun, Mercury and Mars in Aquarius this month which is likely to bedevil all your attempts to find solutions to financial problems, particularly those of a joint or partnership nature, but there is no use moaning that your dilemma is due to other people's unrealistic and irresponsible approach to money. You can only placate the bank manager and plead for extra time to pay your creditors. It may not be any great comfort to be told that all the other eleven signs of the Zodiac are having a miserable time one way or another this February but at least you will know that you are not being singled out for punishment.

AQUARIUS

For many of you February is your birth month, and it is a pity that the astrological picture is such a mess, but Saturn continues to operate in your opposite sign of Leo and there is no escape from matrimonial or partnership conflicts. The real battles are likely to begin after Mars enters Aquarius on the 10th, because you may no longer be prepared to bargain and negotiate for Mars will only strengthen your beliefs and impel you to place all your cards on the table. A word of warning – Saturn is a wily adversary, the great taskmaster and leveller of the Zodiac. Learn to live with it, accept delays, disappointments and frustrations, and ultimately you will achieve greater success and happiness than you ever imagined possible.

PISCES

Not until the Sun enters your own birthsign on February 19 will you begin to feel that you have either personal or career problems in their true perspective, so between the 1st and 18th make the most of what is available and don't pine for what cannot be attained. It's always difficult to define health problems in a general horoscope, but a series of adverse aspects to Saturn in Leo seems to indicate that either you have been burning up far too much physical energy recently or you could be unusually prone to minor ailments. However, ultimately 1977 will prove to be a remarkable and exceptional year for you professionally, and major career changes towards the end of June will bring you the kind of emotional recognition you long for.

JANUARY ~ FEBRUARY

Monday

31

Tuesday
1

Pheasant and partridge shooting ends. Start of salmon fishing season in England and Wales. (Scots must wait another 10 days.)

Wednesday

2

Candlemas Day (when church candles are blessed and distributed). Feast to celebrate presentation of the Infant Christ in the Temple.

Thursday
3

Friday

4

Saturday
5

Another rugby double:
France *v* Wales in Paris;
Ireland *v* England in Dublin.

Sunday

6

Silver Jubilee of the Accession of the Queen in 1952 – she was in a treetop in Kenya at the time. Lots of Jubilee celebrations at home and in Commonwealth. New Zealand National Day.

Supertip
To remove stains from bath make thick cream of equal parts peroxide of hydrogen and cream of tartar. Dab on with sponge and apply two nights running. Very effective.

Supertip
Avoid broken boiled eggs by popping a safety pin into the egg water.

Supertip
To clean the base of an iron that's become stained or sticky, unplug iron and cool, then rub stain with cloth dipped in vinegar or methylated spirits. *Never* try to clean an iron with steel wool, pot scourer or patent abrasive cleaner.

Supertip
If you want to acquire a Coat of Arms then you have to prove descent from an ancestor who is entitled to arms. Apply for help to the Society of Genealogists, 37 Harrington Gardens, London SW7, in order to trace your ancestry. Don't apply to the College of Arms, Queen Victoria Street, London EC4 unless you want a grant of arms, which is expensive to say the least.

Family Favourite

Quick French Onion Soup

Ingredients

1½ lb/675 g large onions
1 oz/25 g butter
1½ pints stock/scant litre (made with chicken or beef cube)
1½ dessertspoons Worcester sauce
salt and pepper
2 oz/50 g grated cheese
French bread

Method

1 Peel and thinly slice onions and fry in butter until golden.
2 Pour stock over onions, add Worcester sauce and seasoning to taste.
3 Simmer gently for 5–10 minutes.
4 Serve in individual bowls (heatproof), topped with slices of French bread sprinkled with grated cheese.
5 Put under a hot grill until cheese is bubbling, then quickly serve.

Gardening

February Gardener

Dig. Dig. Dig. Start a seed box or boxes in a warm kitchen, or buy a propagator: in case you don't know (I didn't), it's a sort of seed incubator and you can let plants grow in it until they're big enough to shove outside (this is called transplanting). Fill propagator with John Innes seed compost.

Sow cauliflower, sprouts, cabbage and leek seeds. Always sow greens in a seed bed or box and then transplant them to give them plenty of room to grow.

Language tip for beginners – You sow a seed and you plant a plant. You can't sow a plant.

Household Hint

With first aid: most people die in accidents during first seven minutes, so move fast.

1 Avoid further damage, turn off power, etc.
2 If victim is unconscious, prevent tongue from blocking airways by tilting head backwards. If no breathing apparent, apply kiss of life.
3 Control bleeding by pressing hard around wound. Apply bandage firmly and raise the bleeding limb.
4 Turn unconscious patient into 'recovery position' – stomach downwards, head sideways, with one knee drawn up and bent. Otherwise patient may choke on own vomit.
5 *Send for help fast.*

FEBRUARY

Monday
7

Charles Dickens's birthday (born 1812).

Tuesday
8

Wednesday
9

Thursday
10

Friday
11

Scottish salmon fishing season starts – they'll be in the shops soon, if you can afford a flake or two.
Crufts Dog Show opens at Olympia, London (until February 12).

Saturday
12

Sunday
13

Supertip
Very good tip for a small boy family! After cleaning bath and sink, dry, then use a clear spray furniture polish to give a dirt-repellent finish.

Supertip
When hanging out or collecting clothes from the line you need your hands free but still want clothes pegs within easy reach. So, hang a loop of tape round your neck and use this for holding the pegs. They can stay on the tape when not in use. Keep on a hook till needed.

Supertip
Ease aching legs and feet when ironing by standing barefoot on a pillow. Iron anything big, such as curtains, on the floor over an old blanket.

Supertip
To lengthen outgrown children's dresses, unpick the hem and use a false hem of ordinary 2-inch (5-cm) cotton bandaging. It's cheap, easy to prepare and lies flat.

Winter Warmer

Kitchen Garden Casserole

Ingredients

4 carrots, peeled and diced
2 onions, peeled and chopped
1 leek, washed and chopped
small cauliflower (divided into florets)
2 oz/50 g plain flour
2 oz/50 g butter
1½ pints/scant litre stock with 1 tablespoon wine vinegar
6–8 spicy sausages, chopped
2 oz/50 g grated Cheddar cheese
salt and pepper

Method

1 Gently cook all vegetables in butter until soft but not mushy (15–20 minutes).
2 Add flour and cook for 2–3 minutes.
3 Gradually add stock, and then sausages.
4 Simmer for further 15–20 minutes; season to taste.
5 Just before serving sprinkle with grated cheese.

Family Favourite

Sweet-Sour Red Cabbage

Ingredients

red cabbage (about 2 lb/900 g)
2 medium onions, peeled and sliced
2 cooking apples, peeled and sliced
2 tablespoons sugar
2 tablespoons port or other dessert wine (or white wine and a dessertspoon redcurrant jelly)
2 tablespoons wine vinegar
bouquet of parsley, thyme, bayleaf
salt and pepper

Method

1 Remove outer leaves of cabbage, cut into quarters, remove core and slice fairly thinly.
2 Arrange in layers in deep earthenware pot alternating with onions and apples.
3 Season as you go with sugar, salt and pepper, and add bouquet, tied with thread, in the middle.
4 When all ingredients are in pot, pour over the wine and vinegar.
5 Cover pot; cook for about 3 hours in a low oven, Mark 2/300°F/150°C.

This can be made a day in advance, because it improves, if anything, with reheating. Goes well with rich dishes such as roast hare, sausages, duck or pork.

FEBRUARY

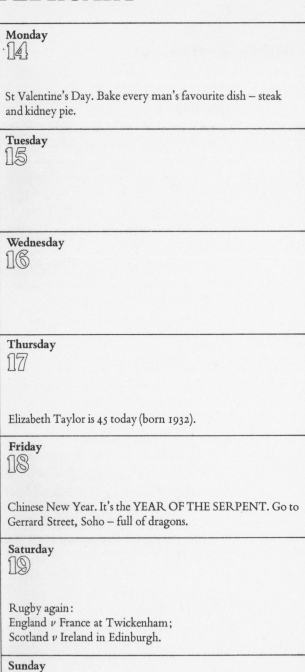

Monday
14

St Valentine's Day. Bake every man's favourite dish – steak
and kidney pie.

Tuesday
15

Wednesday
16

Thursday
17

Elizabeth Taylor is 45 today (born 1932).

Friday
18

Chinese New Year. It's the YEAR OF THE SERPENT. Go to
Gerrard Street, Soho – full of dragons.

Saturday
19

Rugby again:
England *v* France at Twickenham;
Scotland *v* Ireland in Edinburgh.

Sunday
20

Supertip
If you want your laundry to
smell expensive add half a
crumbled bath cube to the final
rinsing water.

Supertip
Cut flowers keep longer and the
water stays clear if you add a
teaspoon of bleach to it.

Traditional Dish

Steak and Kidney Pie
Ingredients
1 lb/450 g skirt or chuck steak
12 oz/350 g ox kidney
8 oz/225 g onion
2 beef stock cubes (Knorr Swiss are best value) melted in 3 tablespoons hot water
good pinch dried thyme
6 oz/175 g mushrooms
2 tablespoons flour
1 teaspoon salt
1 level teaspoon pepper
oil or dripping
8-oz/225-g packet frozen puff pastry

Filling can be cooked the day before, otherwise whole dish takes about 4½ hours to cook, but worth it.

Method
1 Peel and slice onions, then fry in 2 tablespoons oil until golden brown. Place in 3-pint/1¾-litre ovenproof casserole.
2 Mix salt, pepper and flour together.
3 Remove any fat from meat, cut into square cubes and roll in seasoned flour.
4 Fry lightly and put into casserole.
5 Remove core from kidneys, cut into inch cubes, add to casserole.
6 Wash mushrooms, cut two thin slices off the top of each and keep. Chop rest of mushrooms and put into casserole.
7 Add beef stock concentrate and enough water to cover meat.
8 Cook for at least 4 hours at Mark 2/ 300°F/150°C with lid on casserole.
9 After cooking, check seasoning.
10 Place thin slices of raw mushrooms on top of mixture.
11 Make pastry as directed on packet, roll out and put a crust on top of mushrooms. Seal the edges with water.
12 Bake at Mark 8/450°F/230°C for 10 minutes, then reduce temperature to Mark 7/425°F/220°C.
13 Brush top of pastry with beaten egg and cook for further 15–30 minutes.

FEBRUARY

Monday
21

Shrove Monday

Supertip
Make pancakes in advance for Shrove Tuesday (tomorrow). Put a bit of greaseproof paper between each pancake.

Tuesday
22

Shrove Tuesday. (Name comes from the old custom of 'shriving' or making confession the day before the beginning of Lent.)

Astound-your-man department: Traditionally, it's Pancake Day. This year serve them filled with sour cream and caviare (or lumpfish or salmon roe).
For the French it's the festival of Mardi Gras—last chance to have fun before Lent.

Wednesday
23

Ash Wednesday
First day of Lent, which is supposed to be a period of fasting before Easter. Give up giving up.

Name of the day refers to Christian church ceremony when priest dabs ashes, in the sign of the cross, on the foreheads of the congregation. It's 40 days to Easter.

Thursday
24

Friday
25

Supertip
Put a folded newspaper under the doormat to catch all the dirt that goes through. Clean by removing doormat, simply picking up newspaper, folding and throwing away.

Saturday
26

Supertip
Flavour spinach with a pinch of freshly grated nutmeg.

Sunday
27

Supertip
Remove hair lacquer from mirrors, spectacles or bathroom tiles with methylated spirits on a soft cloth.

Family Favourite

Savoury Pancakes and Fillings
Ingredients
6 oz/175 g flour
1 egg
½ pint/3 dl milk
cooking fat
good pinch salt to taste

Fillings (Fried in a separate pan. Quantities given for 4 good fillings)
- 4 oz/100 g minced meat, 1 finely chopped large onion, pinch of thyme
- 2 oz/50 g chicken livers mixed with chopped onion
- 2 oz/50 g chopped mushrooms and 2 rashers chopped bacon
- 1 gill/1½ dl sour cream mixed with a 2-oz/50-g jar of lumpfish roe

Method
1 Place flour and salt in deep bowl, break egg into the middle, beat, slowly adding milk until mixture has thick creamy consistency.
2 Melt fat in medium-sized frying pan until smoking hot, then add enough mixture to cover *thinly* the bottom of the pan.
3 Do not let the pancake stick; move constantly, then turn over and cook reverse side.
4 When brown on both sides, add filling and serve.

If possible leave batter mixture for half an hour before using.

Reputation Maker

Jugged Hare
Ingredients
4–5 lb/2–2¼ kg hare, jointed
3 tablespoons flour
2 onions, peeled and sliced
1½ oz/40 g bacon dripping
1 pint/6 dl stock
1 mug red cooking wine
¼ lb/100 g diced bacon
¼ teaspoon ground cloves
4 tablespoons mixed herbs
½ teaspoon mace
salt and pepper

Method
1 Flour the pieces of hare and brown them in the bacon dripping.
2 Remove when browned, add onions to pan and brown them.
3 Add bacon.
4 Put the hare back in the pan, and add stock and wine, mixed herbs, cloves, mace and seasoning.
5 Bring to boil and simmer gently for 2–3 hours, or until tender. Do not overcook. Serve with redcurrant jelly.

Traditionally, liquor is thickened with the blood of the hare, but the squeamish can use flour.

March

ARIES

During the first three weeks of March you will be picking up a lot of pieces and trying to fit them together to make a composite picture of emotional problems. One thing is certain, there won't be quite so many dramas and dreary hours spent alone. Your ruler Mars has passed the opposition point to Saturn and you can look forward to a more tranquil and reassuring phase ahead. In fact, because Venus remains in your own birthsign until the beginning of June you stand a better chance of getting partners and loved ones to agree that although you may be impulsive and headstrong, you do at least tell the truth. Joint finances and business affairs, however, have got to be approached with total honesty, and even then the bank manager will be difficult to convince.

TAURUS

Although the Sun in Pisces is fairly well aspected between March 1 and 20, and new friendships and personal relationships will prevent you from being too downcast and despondent, Saturn in Leo is at an adverse angle to the revolutionary planet Uranus in your opposite sign of Scorpio, so it must follow that this will be a month when you will have to face up to challenging conditions in your home and family life and anticipate an unusual number of conflicts with partners. Saturn is in retrograde motion, and you in turn will seem to be covering a lot of old ground and continually being drawn back into the past until a permanent solution can be found.

GEMINI

You fare no better and no worse than anyone else this month. Exceedingly good aspects relate to work and career prospects throughout the whole of March, but you are just going to have to put up with relatives who interfere and continually criticize. At the beginning of next month the great benefactor Jupiter enters Gemini, where it will stay until late August, and you will be able to blaze new trails, feel supremely self-confident and find your feelings reciprocated. So you can afford to be that much more generous and magnanimous now knowing that everything is on the up and up. Gemini's tool is the mind, the rational mind to be more specific. The mind, however, must be opened a little at a time. Too much high voltage will blow it.

CANCER

Sadly, Saturn in Leo continues to play havoc with finances, and although there should be a slight improvement in joint arrangements and business affairs this March, it would be very unwise indeed to take any chances whatsoever which could jeopardize your earning power and security. This said, the overall picture is a much more encouraging one. The Sun in Pisces until the 20th is at a beautiful angle to your natal Sun in Cancer, and it's time you got out of a rut. Pack your bags and contemplate life and its day-to-day problems for a while in more harmonious and picturesque surroundings. Cancerian ladies are always presented as over-anxious, over-protective, clucking mother hens, but there is a calculating streak. Fear of revealing yourself often prevents acquisition of knowledge.

LEO

As you must live with Saturn in Leo for the next couple of years, perhaps this is the right moment to sort a few things out and put you straight, once and for all. Saturn suggests the character, a word which sums up and summarizes the amount of reserve force, mental, emotional and spiritual, accumulated by the individual during the experience of a lifetime. Everything you now take in hand requires a good deal of patience and perseverance; the tendency is to pay more attention to what is considered to be bad rather than good luck. However, if you are really intuitive and perceptive you will learn a great deal about prudence, perseverance, steadfastness, tact, method and reliability, and still have a lot of fun.

VIRGO

You are now about to reach some crossroads or turning point in your life. The Sun in Pisces occupies a position totally opposed to your birthsign, and it will probably be in the area of partnerships, either of an emotional or practical nature, that you have to decide once and for all whether or not current relationships are valid and worth pursuing. Much will be revealed in a roundabout or indirect way since Saturn is adversely aspected by the unconventional and uncompromising planet Uranus, and you are bound at some point or other to be disillusioned. Take heart – Jupiter is about to enter the midheaven of your solar horoscope and your career or professional prospects haven't been quite so good for almost 12 years.

LIBRA

There is one particular adverse planetary aspect between Saturn and Uranus which seems to indicate that you haven't yet managed to stabilize your finances – even if you have tried, which is doubtful, you haven't tried quite hard enough. This is not a month for excuses, or endeavouring to explain that everything would be lovely if friends repaid the money they owed; your only alternative is to get out there and glitter, and boost your income by working harder. March is a month of incredible opportunities as far as your career prospects are concerned. At times, the Sun, Mercury and Mars will all be in Pisces, so get off the fence, use your imagination and make others realize you are about to tilt the scales in your own favour.

SCORPIO

Now you enter a tricky phase of the year, when Uranus in Scorpio is blocked or challenged by Saturn, and you must take a deep breath, curb your impatience and plan a new campaign. It is, however, a fantastic month for romance and affairs of the heart, but for once you are probably more concerned with pursuing your career aims and ambitions than finding someone who satisfies your emotional needs. No one knows better than you what it is you want to achieve but what you must ensure now is that your timing is right, or, to be more precise, that you don't mistime your actions. Saturn in the midheaven of your solar horoscope brings you in closer contact with people who can and would help, but the methods they use may appear to be old-fashioned and outmoded.

SAGITTARIUS

At the beginning of April your ruler Jupiter will enter your opposite sign of Gemini; in the meantime you must work out a plan or formula which enables you to find a way to remove any remaining obstacles or conflicts which would prevent you from working in total harmony with partners. The Sun in Pisces until March 20 accentuates the areas of conflict and discord in your home life or within the family. You should, however, begin to feel that a lot of the problems which arose in the past were due to misunderstandings, miscalculations and hurt pride. Perhaps a quote from Goethe is applicable now – 'One need only grow older to become milder in one's judgement; I see no error committed which I have not also committed.'

CAPRICORN

You don't have to be bowed down or beaten by current planetary transits, and even though your own ruler Saturn is adversely aspected by the unconventional and revolutionary planet Uranus, making partnership finances and business dealings an absolute nightmare, Pluto in your area of personal and professional prestige indicates that what matters most is that you continue to consolidate your position and learn from your experiences. Capricorns always know they have a lot to learn and a lot to experience, but somehow family ties and responsibilities prevent you from finding the time and the opportunity to indulge yourself. There are always things to be done, schedules to be kept to, obligations and commitments to be fulfilled.

AQUARIUS

It's not money, or mortgages, or problems of a material nature that will flummox you this month. In fact, you should be surprisingly well off for a change. But, because your own ruling planet Uranus in Scorpio is adversely aspected by Saturn, you are expected to value and appreciate partnerships and relationships. Aquarius is a peculiar sign and an unpredictable one. You are absolutely marvellous when others expect you to be monstrous and monstrous when you are expected to be marvellous. What you can never be is taken for granted. Aquarius is above all the Truth Seeker. The Water Bearer gives freely but somehow fails to appreciate the simple needs of those close at hand, more specifically the family.

PISCES

No need to pull the poor Pisces routine this month. The Sun's in your birthsign, you are mentally that much more alert, intuitively accurate and emotionally secure. In fact the only problems you are likely to encounter will be in deciding which of the many career opportunities you should accept. The answer is none. Wait until the Sun enters Aries on March 21, when unusually favourable aspects relate to personal finances, rather than settling for anything which is offered now. An adverse aspect between Saturn and Uranus this March may force you to curtail or postpone travel plans. However, after Mars enters your own birthsign on March 21 nothing can really phase or flummox you, nor can anyone undermine your confidence.

Monday
28

Plan spring cleaning countdown. Shop for cleaning materials.

Tuesday
1

Feast of St David, patron saint of Wales.
Bookings open for new Shakespeare season at Stratford on Avon. Season starts April 1.

Wednesday
2

Thursday
3

Friday
4

Saturday
5

More big rugby matches:
Wales *v* England at Cardiff;
France *v* Scotland at Edinburgh.
Have steaming casserole ready for when they return frozen.

Sunday
6

Supertip
Peel onions painlessly in a bowl of cold water.

Winter Warmer

Carrot Soup

Ingredients

1½ lb/675 g carrots, peeled and sliced
½ lb/225 g tomatoes, chopped
1½ pints/scant litre chicken stock
¼ pint/1½ dl milk
¼ pint/1½ dl single cream
2 oz/50 g butter
pinch of chervil
chopped parsley
salt and pepper

Method

1 Gently cook the carrots in melted butter for 3–4 minutes, add tomatoes and cook for further 4 minutes.

2 Add heated stock and chervil to carrots and tomatoes, season, cover pan and simmer until carrots are tender (about 30 minutes).

3 Put through blender or sieve, return to pan and add the milk and cream.

4 Heat, but do not boil the soup, correct seasoning and serve hot, garnished with chopped parsley.

Gardening

March Gardener

Many vegetable seeds can be sown outdoors from now on: start with broad beans, peas, parsnips. Plant leeks, shallots and onion sets (which are onions already partly grown).
New lawns can be sown.
Established lawns can enjoy a first mowing, if you must.

Tips from the grass roots

If you can't seem to grow grass, buy a general-purpose shade grass seed which has been anti-bird treated. It costs 55p per lb (£1.20 per kg) from a nursery and you allow 1–2 oz (25–50 g) per square yard of bald earth. Then rake up lawn, ignoring existing grass, which will look messy for a few days, before springing to life. Hose well after sowing.

To preserve cut flowers in water

Daffodils, other bulb flowers and thin stems: Cut 1 inch (2½ cm) off stem.
Hard-stemmed flowers: Bash bottom 4 inches (10 cm) of stems, or they can't absorb water.
Roses: Gently remove any damaged petals and strip off thorns from stem. Split or crush stem end with steak hammer, heel of shoe, etc. Scrape off stems for first 6 inches (15 cm). Plunge to neck in cold water.
To revive a wilting flower arrangement: Snip off ends of stems and stand in 1 inch (2½ cm) of boiling water for a few seconds, then give the flowers a long drink up to the neck in cold water for a few hours.

MARCH

Monday
7

Tuesday
8

International Women's Day.
Daily Mail Ideal Home Exhibition opens at Olympia, London.
Chelsea Antiques Fair.

Wednesday
9

Thursday
10

Friday
11

Saturday
12

Football League Cup Final at Wembley.

Sunday
13

Next Sunday is Mothering Sunday, if you want to write her a letter and can afford to post it.

Motherlore
Don't put it down, put it away.

I hear that Tampax have received a letter from an Irishman in Dublin as follows: 'Dear Sir, I have been using your product for 5 years but am still not able to ride, swim or play tennis. Would you please advise me what I'm doing wrong.'

Winter Warmer

Antonia's Goulash

Ingredients

2 lb/900 g stewing beef
1 lb/450 g onions, chopped
2 teaspoons caraway seeds
paprika
salt
1 gill/1½ dl sour cream
1 oz/25 g butter
2 cloves garlic, peeled and crushed
¾ pint/4½ dl stock.

Method

1 Cut beef into bite-sized pieces.
2 Use a deep fireproof casserole. Fry onions in butter until soft. Add steak which has been rolled in seasoned flour.
3 When steak is browned add caraway seeds, salt, garlic and stock.
4 Cover with thick layer of paprika but do not mix in or it will burn.
5 Cook in a low oven Mark 3/325°F/160°C for 1½ hours or until meat is tender.
6 Serve with sour cream, baked potatoes and chives.

Traditional Dish

Poor Man's Cassoulet

Ingredients

½ lb/225 g streaky pork (salt or otherwise)
1 lb/450 g haricot beans
1 large onion, peeled and sliced
2 tablespoons black treacle
dash of Worcester sauce
1 dessertspoon brown sugar
1 dessertspoon dry mustard
salt and pepper

Method

1 Soak haricot beans overnight, then cook for 1½–2 hours in the water in which they were soaked.
2 Strain beans and keep the water.
3 Cut pork into bite-sized pieces.
4 Heat bean water and make sauce by stirring in treacle, mustard, sugar, Worcester sauce, salt and pepper.
5 Mix beans, onions and meat in a casserole; add sauce, which should just cover the beans.
6 Cover casserole and bake in moderate oven Mark 4/350°F/180°C for about 1 hour, or until the beans are soft but not mushy.
7 Add more water if beans absorb all moisture before they are cooked.

MARCH

Monday
14

Freshwater coarse fishing season ends.

Tuesday
15

Wednesday
16

Thursday
17

St Patrick's Day, Festival of the patron saint of Ireland (where it's a Bank Holiday).
Make a traditional potato pie.

Friday
18

Saturday
19

Pick daffodils for Mother's Day (tomorrow).
Yet another big rugby double date:
Ireland *v* France at Dublin;
Scotland *v* Wales at Edinburgh.

Sunday
20

First day of spring (the Vernal Equinox)
British Summer Time begins. Clocks forward 1 hour.
Mothering Sunday.

Motherlore
Of course it's unfair, everything is (if said firmly this will avoid 30% of arguments between brothers and sisters, and realistically equip them for life).

Motherlore
If you put it on the floor you must expect it to be trodden on by clumsy grownups.

Supertip
Save old toothbrushes for fiddly jobs like cleaning round tap bottoms, patterned silverware, carved furniture and the tops of skirting boards.

Motherlore
Give nothing to the card, telegram or flower industry. Give her breakfast in bed, or see she gets a newsy letter.

Traditional Dish

Potato Pie

Ingredients
2 lb/900 g potatoes
2 onions, peeled and finely chopped
1 oz/25 g butter
½ lb/225 g Cheddar cheese, grated
3 eggs
½ pint/3 dl milk
salt and pepper
chopped parsley, to taste

Method
1 Boil potatoes. When cooked and slightly cooled, peel and dice them.
2 Cook onions gently in the butter until soft and transparent.
3 Mix potatoes, onions, cheese and parsley together and spread in an ovenproof dish.
4 In a separate bowl, beat eggs, stir in milk and pour over potato mixture.
5 Bake in moderate oven Mark 4/ 350°F/180°C for about 30 minutes.
6 Serve by itself, or with a crisp green salad.

Reputation Maker

How to Make One Family-sized Chicken Serve 14 Contented People

I've never heard anyone complain. Nobody believes this until they've seen it. I was taught to dismember my birds by a French farmer's wife.

First, invest in a pair of poultry shears; they will have paid for themselves after about 6 birds.

Secondly, roast the bird as usual, giving it an extra sprinkle of salt 5 minutes before removing from oven.

Portions
2 Remove the wings, cutting round the shoulder blades. (The shoulder blades are the only important things to remember, professionals call them wing joints.)
4 Now cut each leg in two.
Now cut the bird in two, horizontally; imagine a plimsoll line around its middle.
4 Vertically cut the top of the carcass into 4 pieces.
4 Vertically cut the bottom of the carcass into 4.

MARCH

Monday
21

Tuesday
22

Wednesday
23

Thursday
24

Friday
25

Feast of the Annunciation, when the Angel Gabriel brought the Virgin Mary the message that she would bear a son, Jesus Christ. Flat racing season starts.

Saturday
26

Sunday
27

Supertip
If you've made your soup too salty, drop in a piece of raw potato and let it boil in the soup for a few minutes. Then remove the potato and you'll find it will have absorbed most of the surplus salt.

To make a lemon last longer: If you just want a squeeze of lemon juice for a recipe, don't cut the lemon. Just prick it with a fork and squeeze.

To avoid spills: When carrying medicines downstairs some hospital nurses sing 'Here Comes the Bride' under their breath.

Supertip
If you can't open a bottle top or jar with your bare hands – try
1 gripping it with a nutcracker;
2 heating lid under a running hot tap, to expand the metal;
3 winding rubber bands round the lid tightly in order to get a firm handgrip.

Family Favourite

Cream of Tomato Soup
Ingredients

1½ lb/675 g peeled tomatoes

2 oz/50 g peeled, chopped onion

2 oz/50 g peeled, chopped carrot

1 oz/25 g butter

1 pint/6 dl water or stock

1 bayleaf

2 lumps sugar

pinch of mace or nutmeg

salt and pepper

3–4 tablespoons cream or evaporated milk

a few chopped chives (optional)

Method

1 Brown onion and carrot in butter.

2 Remove from heat and stir in flour.

3 Add pulped tomatoes, stock or water, bayleaf, sugar, spice and seasoning.

4 Stir until boiling.

5 Simmer for 20 minutes.

6 Add cream and chopped chives.

Reputation Maker

Mushroom Salad
Ingredients

1 lb/450 g button mushrooms, washed and thinly sliced

1 gill/1½ dl French dressing

1 handful chopped parsley

Method

1 Wash and slice mushrooms thinly.

2 Souse mushrooms in French dressing and leave to soak overnight (or mushrooms will not absorb enough dressing and will taste spongy).

3 Mix in chopped parsley before serving.

Family Favourite

Chicory and Orange Salad
Ingredients

2 large heads chicory

1 large orange, peeled and sliced

1 oz/25 g walnuts

French dressing

Method

1 Trim chicory of any discoloured bits, chop off base and separate leaves, wash, drain and dry.

2 Toss ingredients in French dressing and serve.

April

ARIES

The Sun in your own sign of Aries until April 20 makes the best possible aspects to Saturn and Neptune, which should strengthen and sustain you when partners play up again and put both your emotions and loyalty to the test. Mercury in Taurus after the 4th turns to retrograde motion on the 20th, implying that finances, especially earnings, won't live up to expectation. Since 1971 Pluto has been passing through your opposite sign of Libra; this planet is the most recently discovered of the Sun's cosmic family and the most mysterious. It can best be described as 'The Transformer'. It is destructive only to construct. No wonder then that you tend to question relationships more and in some instances feel you have outgrown them.

TAURUS

You will probably be spending an unusual amount of time alone this April, mainly because you won't have either the energy or the desire to battle until the Sun enters your own birthsign on April 21. Even then, you will tend to mull over problems rather than force issues out into the open. A Taurian realizes that it takes a long time for an acorn to become an oak tree. You first like to make sure that the roots are embedded in the ground, and you are right. The planetary set-up at the moment seems to suggest that both partnership and family difficulties have built up over a long period and no matter how hard you try a permanent solution depends on the willingness of others to co-operate.

GEMINI

Jupiter enters your own birthsign on April 4 and you begin to feel more optimistic and self-reliant, with a greater thirst for change and travel. First, however, you must set about re-establishing the right kind of relationship with those you profess to love. You have probably been branded as sceptical, talkative and unreliable recently, and some major adverse planetary aspects in your solar horoscope suggest that you are liable to be out of favour both at home and at work. However, Jupiter, like Venus, is the planet of good fortune, and between now and late August it's simply a question of choosing your words carefully and proving that your emotions and devotions are for real.

CANCER

Cancer is the fourth sign of the Zodiac, and in simple astrology relates to the home, family and security. It is necessary for you to find the right place where you can reminisce, dream, create and feel safe. However, this month's planetary movements highlight career and professional interests in a rather spectacular way and you are bound to be hauled over the coals because you can't devote sufficient time to resolving dreary domestic problems. Others don't seem to give a fig that you must also have some kind of personal success and recognition. They want you close at hand to sort out their finances, to discuss their emotions, and to be some kind of a buffer. Tell them it's time they learnt to fend for themselves.

LEO

Between April 1 and 20 the Sun in Aries enables you to look way beyond present restrictions and limitations, and focuses your attention on matters, places and people which stimulate your imagination. Career issues are also highlighted because of the presence of Mercury in Taurus. However, this planet turns to retrograde motion on the 20th, so unless you have finalized agreements or signed contracts prior to this date, hold fire until mid May, otherwise you could be hopelessly misled or deceived. Jupiter in Gemini after April 4 implies that you are about to enter an entire new cycle in friendships and very close associations. Leos may have strong hearts physically and weak ones emotionally, but now it is to be hoped that your sincerity and generosity will be reciprocated.

VIRGO

Not until Mars moves out of your opposite sign of Pisces on April 28 can you hope to find any real peace of mind or permanent solutions to matrimonial or partnership problems. Mars in opposition makes others unwilling to compromise, which is a rather nice way of saying that they badger and berate you at the slightest provocation. And they certainly won't understand your anxieties over finances. However, there is one planetary movement this month which could turn the tide of fortune well in your favour. Jupiter in Gemini after the 4th transits the midheaven point of your solar horoscope, so you should find yourself several rungs higher up the ladder to fame and recognition.

LIBRA

Librans are born charmers – they instinctively know how to make someone feel desired. Librans are also natural romantics, always searching for the perfect partner because they loathe being alone. There is another facet of the Libran nature which does not like to see any form of reality that is unpleasant, and anything heavy or depressing has to be covered up or concealed. The only way to escape the unpleasant reality which now pervades partnerships is by taking a trip or an early holiday, whether or not you can afford one. In fact, with Jupiter in your angle of long-distance travel after April 4 it might not be a bad idea to pack your bags. Both personal and partnership finances remain confused, but then you never really expect them to be otherwise.

SCORPIO

The challenging aspect between Uranus in Scorpio and Saturn in Leo continues to put you on your mettle and make you that much more determined not only to find your right niche at work, but also to confound others by your resilience and resourcefulness. However, you would be very misguided indeed if you entered into new agreements after Mercury turns to retrograde motion in your opposite sign of Taurus on April 20. In fact for a period of three weeks from this date, all partnerships, ties and alliances will prove worthless in the long run. However, there are a couple of cheery aspects to Jupiter in your angle of joint money matters and business affairs this month, so at least you will be able to cry in comfort.

SAGITTARIUS

The most significant planetary factor this month relates to your own ruler Jupiter, which from the 4th takes up a position in your opposite sign of Gemini. This can mean one of two things; either you will find that partners and loved ones change their tactics and become that much more open and direct, or, alternatively, you will begin to see exactly where the areas of differences and conflicts lie. In any event, even long-term plans will have to be changed, and your efforts will be channelled towards resolving problems of a very personal nature rather than those related to your job and security. Sagittarius is considered to be a fortunate sign, and you certainly inspire confidence in others, but aren't you perhaps too easily deflated and thrown off course?

CAPRICORN

As a Capricorn, you tend to attach too much importance to externals, not necessarily for bad reasons but because being born under the last Earth sign you firmly believe that financial and material security is a must. Professionally, you should have no cause for complaint. Jupiter in your angle of work after the 4th makes a stunning aspect to Pluto in the midheaven of your solar birthchart, and you will undoubtedly impress those who matter by your abilities and practical approach to problems. However, you are not on such firm ground when it comes to domestic issues and relationships with the rest of the family. You are never as cool, calculating and dispassionate as others imagine but you can only change their opinions by showing your true emotions.

AQUARIUS

An extraordinary breadth of vision and an absolutely unbiased open mind are supposed to be the attributes of the true Aquarian. But now, with Saturn so adversely aspected in your opposite sign of Leo, you can be forgiven for wondering if you have been too tolerant, sympathetic and compromising with partners, loved ones and colleagues. The answer is no, and you must continue to stick to your ideals and principles no matter how much others thwart and antagonize you. Saturn is the great teacher of the Zodiac and what you are about to learn is that instead of crusading for friends and associates you should be taking a greater interest in what is going on close to home.

PISCES

At their supreme best, Pisceans can achieve a realization of the essential unity of all things that is overwhelming. You are born poets, dreamers of beautiful and chimerical dreams. It's the reality bit you find difficult, and the reality this month is that you have just got to learn to be self-sufficient and more practical. Mars in Pisces until the 28th is a great help, for it makes you that much more energetic and self-confident. Between the 1st and 20th, the Sun in Aries accentuates the importance of what you earn, and the way in which you handle income and finances. Don't on any account allow others to impose on your generosity or influence your judgement. Isn't it about time partners and close associates also told the truth?

Monday

28

Supertip
Quickest way to make hot toast cold is to air it in a toast rack. So why not wrap it in a pretty napkin and pass it round?

Tuesday
29

Wednesday
30

How to get drink stains off marble
Wipe the stain off as soon as possible. Leave anything else till the next morning but as soon as the last guest has gone wipe wine or spirit stains off a marble table or fireplace.
A mild abrasive such as Vim should remove stains, but, if not, try a little lemon juice or vinegar. This must be rinsed off immediately, then dried and polished.

Thursday
31

Financial Year 1976–77 ends.

Friday
1

April Fool's Day – watch out.
New Shakespeare season opens at Stratford on Avon.
Postal bookings open for Glyndebourne Festival Opera.

Saturday

2

Motherlore
The Passover is 'the feast of unleavened bread' – an eight-day season of rejoicing and happiness celebrating the deliverance of the Children of Israel from Egyptian slavery and their exodus from Egypt. During Passover Jews do not eat bread or anything which is leavened. Instead crispy matzos are served.

Grand National Day. Very dangerous for horses.
Prêt à porter collections open in Paris. Don't bother to go.
Buy *Elle*.

Sunday

3

Jewish Passover starts.
Palm Sunday. This commemorates Christ's arrival in triumph in Jerusalem, when the crowd strewed palms before him.

Today Christian churches will be decorated with branches of palm – or willow.

Family Favourite

Cream of Peas Monaco.
A great favourite of ex-Queen Alexandra of Yugoslavia

Ingredients
- 1 lb/450 g frozen peas
- 2 pints/generous litre hot beef stock or tinned consommé
- ½ pint/3 dl cream
- pinch of sugar
- salt and pepper
- 1 oz/25 g butter
- 1 tablespoon chopped red pimento

Method
1. Cook peas quickly in salted water, strain and sieve.
2. Add peas to hot stock, then add cream, sugar and seasoning.
3. Heat thoroughly, but do not allow to boil.
4. Add butter, whisking as it melts.
5. Garnish with pimento and serve.

Traditional Dish

Ena Sharples's Lancashire Roughened Potatoes

Ingredients.
- 2 lb/900 g potatoes
- 2 oz/50 g butter
- salt and pepper

Method
1. Scrub potatoes and boil in salted water, leaving skins on.
2. When cooked, divide into four and quickly add butter to hot saucepan, allowing 2 oz/50 g butter per 2 lb/900 g potatoes (yes, I know it's a lot).
3. Add *lots* of freshly ground black pepper. The trick is to melt the butter first and smash the potatoes as little as possible so that they look . . . just roughened.

Household Hint

Sprinkle savoury dishes with parsley or paprika. Garnish with lemon slices or a couple of cucumber slices or 4 prawns (at either end of the dish), or 6 dotted olives or a sprig of watercress in the middle. Don't turn up your nose at the word 'garnish'. It means making a dish look either less dull or more grand or both.

If you've got a dull-looking cake or pudding for a rather festive grand occasion – stick a flower on it. I've successfully used one white chrysanthemum head on a white iced cake and a small group of daisies on a Victoria sponge. Use whatever flower is to hand in vase, hedge or backyard.

APRIL

Monday
4

Easter school holiday about to start.
Plan some family outings.

Supertip
Old-fashioned straight potato peelers can be used for digging weeds out of the lawn.

Tuesday
5

Last chance to have a baby before Income Tax Year ends.
Most schools break up for Easter this week.

Wednesday
6

Supertip
Easter lamb expensive if home-grown. Chicken or small turkey may be better buy. Boiled or baked ham useful at holiday time.

Thursday
7

Maundy Thursday, the anniversary of the Last Supper.
Queen carries out ancient royal Maundy ceremony of handing specially coined silver money to old men and women.

Motherlore
This was the day when Christ told his disciples to love one another and washed their feet.

Friday
8

Good Friday.   Bank Holiday.
Prepare eggs for Sunday. Hardboil then paint on little faces or flowers.

Motherlore
This is the day Christ was crucified on the cross at Calvary. It's called Good Friday because Christians believe this day marks their salvation (in some countries it's called Black Friday).

Saturday
9

Lent ends at midnight tonight.

Easter and other holidays
Here's an excellent way to make a stale loaf taste new again. Simply hold it under a running tap for a few seconds, give it a shake, then put in moderate oven for 10 minutes or until it feels crisp. You can now overbuy bread supplies at holiday time without the risk of some of it going stale.

Sunday
10

Easter Day. Celebration of Christ's Resurrection from the dead. The Easter Parade in Battersea Park, London – lots of massed bands.

Gardening

April Gardener
Sow more seeds out of doors, including peas, beetroot, turnips. Plant main crop potatoes.

Weed, weed, weed, to prevent weeds seeding.

Traditional Dish

Hot Cross Buns (Makes 12–16 buns)
Ingredients
½ pint/3 dl warm milk
1 lb/450 g plain flour
½ oz/15 g yeast
1 teaspoon sugar
1 teaspoon salt
¾ oz/22 g lard
2 oz/50 g sugar
1 teaspoon spice
2 oz/50 g sultanas

Glaze
2 tablespoons sugar
2 tablespoons water

Method
1 Cream yeast and sugar until liquid, then add milk.
2 Sprinkle a little flour on top, cover and put in a warm place for about 15 minutes until it begins to rise.
3 Sift the remaining flour into a warm bowl, with the salt.
4 Rub in the lard.
5 Add sugar, fruit and spice, then stir in yeast mixture.
6 If necessary, add more milk to make a soft dough.
7 Knead well.
8 Cover and leave to rise until doubled in size.
9 Knead lightly, shape into bun shapes and put on a greased baking tray.
10 On top of each bun cut a cross with a sharp knife and leave to rise until double the size.
11 Bake until buns sound hollow when tapped on the bottom.
Mark 7/425°F/220°C.
12 While still hot, brush with a glaze made by mixing sugar and water then bringing it to the boil.

APRIL

Monday
11

Easter Monday. Bank Holiday (but not in Scotland).
Carthorse Parade in Regent's Park, London (strongly
recommended).

Tuesday
12

Wednesday
13

Thursday
14

Remember to buy birthday card for Queen.

Friday
15

Saturday
16

Sunday
17

Supertip
Instead of serving mashed
potatoes, why not: Thinly slice
some potatoes and onions, put in
a fireproof dish and bake in a hot
oven for 1 hour. Beat two eggs
with salt, pepper and a cupful of
cream and pour over vegetables.
Sprinkle with grated cheese and
bake in a hot oven for 15
minutes.

Supertip
You probably won't believe it,
but you can make a deliciously
refreshing drink with a nice zing
to it by adding a few drops of
angostura bitters to chilled soda
water.

Motherlore
Always finish any redecorating
job half an hour before you
planned to do so. You always try
to do half an hour too much.

Household Hint

How do you unplug an aerosol which is hissing feebly but not squirting?

1 Give the can a good shake to unblock any possible blockage.
2 Take the button off the aerosol and rinse under the tap. Poke a pin through the little hole. If it's a blocked paint aerosol soak the button in paint solvent.
3 Check that the tube on which the button fits is clean and unblocked.
4 Replace button firmly.

5 For things like spray starch, try not to turn the can upside down to spray – keep at about a 45° angle – otherwise you may find that you're just letting all the gas propellant out.
6 When you're getting to the end of the supply try twiddling the top button around a bit, which in turn will move the tube around, and you'll probably find you get two or three more good squirts out.

Family Favourite

Soda Bread

In case you run out. Takes only an hour to make and bake, with 3 added advantages:

(a) You don't need yeast
(b) You don't have to knead the dough
(c) You don't have to wait for 20 minutes for the dough to rise.

Ingredients

1 lb/450 g wholemeal flour
1 teaspoon salt
1 teaspoon bicarbonate of soda
6–8 fl oz/2–2½ dl sour milk or buttermilk
butter

Method

1 Grease a large baking sheet with butter, and preheat oven to Mark 7/ 425°F/220°C.
2 Put the flour, salt and bicarbonate of soda into mixing bowl and gradually beat in 6 fl oz/2 dl of sour milk or buttermilk with a wooden spoon. The mixture should be smooth and firm – if necessary add more milk.
3 Place the dough on a floured board and shape into a round flat loaf about 8 inches/21 cm in diameter.
4 Place the loaf on the greased baking sheet, take a sharp knife and cut a deep cross on the top of the loaf.
5 Bake for 30–35 minutes, when the top should be golden brown.

Monday
18

Tuesday
19

Wednesday
20

Thursday
21

H.M. the Queen's birthday.
She is 51 today.

Friday
22

Saturday
23

St George's Day. Feast of the patron saint of England, on the anniversary of his martyrdom in 303.
Shakespeare's anniversary. It was his birthday in 1564 and he died on this day in 1616.

Sunday
24

Try on bikini, plan diet.
School holidays end this week.

Supertip
Remember the importance of the plumber's mate. Do-it-yourselfers and otherwise must remember that doing any household maintenance work, from the tedious little chore to repainting the living room, is easier if you have someone else with you. Someone to spur you on, cheer you up, patch you up and wipe you down – ideally, of course, someone to complete the job for you.

Supertip
Old Mother Conran's window cleaning recipe: Mix one cup paraffin, one cup water and one cup methylated spirit. Shake well in bottle, rub on glass, polish off when dry. Also good for cleaning piano keys.

Motherlore
Blessed are the pure in heart but they don't have much to talk about.

Supertip
If your place is too small, e.g. a bedsitter, keep it uncluttered (where do you put the clutter? – under the bed, of course). Use one colour scheme throughout, even for the floor covering, because it suggests space, calm and continuity. I keep on telling people this and they never do it.

Traditional Dish

Flora MacDonald's Shortbread

Ingredients
6–8 oz/175–225 g plain flour
4 oz/100 g butter
2 oz/50 g caster sugar
pinch of salt

Method
1 Cream butter and sugar together until light and fluffy.
2 Gradually stir in flour with a fork.
3 Draw mixture together with finger-tips.
4 Press into two 6-inch (15-cm) rounds and prick well.
5 Bake until pale brown at Mark 3/ 325°F/160°C for about ¾ hour.
6 Cut into pieces while still warm.

Reputation Maker

Consommé with Caviare

Ingredients
2 tins Crosse & Blackwell's consommé
2 sherry glasses of sherry
juice of ½ lemon
pepper
4 tablespoons fresh or sour cream
4 dollops mock caviare (lumpfish roe)

Method
Melt consommé gently in saucepan, add sherry and lemon juice and pepper. Rejell in fridge and serve cold, broken up in individual bowls, topped with a little fresh or sour cream and a dollop of mock caviare.

Family Favourite

The Savoy Club Sandwich

Ingredients (for 1 sandwich)
2 slices toast
2 leaves shredded lettuce
4 slices white chicken meat
3 slices grilled bacon
4 slices peeled tomato
4 slices egg
1 dessertspoon mayonnaise

Method
1 Collect all ingredients together.
2 Mix salad with mayonnaise and spread the mixture on one side of each slice of toast. Pile all the other ingredients on to just 1 piece of toast, then put the other slice on top.
3 Put in a moderate oven to warm for 2–3 minutes and serve quickly.

Monday
25

English Bach Festival opens in London for 2 weeks, then a week in Oxford.

Tuesday
26

Wednesday
27

Thursday
28

Friday
29

Saturday
30

Fly to Moscow for May Day Parade.
Royal Academy Summer Exhibition opens.

Sunday
1

May Day.
Trade Union marches. Very impressive. All those banners.
You can't eat oysters from now till August.
Cricket season starts with first John Player League games.

Good way to save money on tablet soap is to buy the bath size and cut into 4 pieces. As with mustard, what makes the soap makers' fortunes is the soap that isn't used but melted in the bath!

Savoury Bread Pudding
Make a bread and butter pudding in the usual way, but instead of fruit and sugar substitute grated cheese and sliced raw onion between the bread and butter layers.

For young children's parties
How to make your own ice lollies:
Make up strawberry or chocolate milkshake with powder and milk. Pour into ice-cube tray and freeze until almost firm. Put a cocktail stick into each and freeze overnight.

Supertip
If buying vacuum bags irritates you as much as it does me, try saving the rubber bands from packages and any ordinary plastic bags without holes that come your way. I attach the plastic bag to the suction inlet with the rubber bands. I know somebody else who simply pushes those long plastic bread bags into her vacuum bags. Yet another job eliminated.

Family Favourite

Egg and Potato Casserole

Ingredients

1 lb/450 g potatoes, peeled and diced
2 tablespoons butter
2 tablespoons olive oil
¼ Spanish onion, peeled and finely chopped
6 eggs
4 tablespoons grated Gruyère cheese
1 gill/1½ dl double cream
salt and pepper

Method

1 Heat olive oil and butter in frying pan, then fry potatoes until they begin to change colour.
2 Add onion and continue to cook until potatoes are properly cooked.
3 Season generously.
4 Put cooked potatoes and onion in the bottom of an ovenproof gratin dish.
5 Break eggs carefully over potatoes and sprinkle with cheese.
6 Cover with cream and season again.
7 Cook in a moderate oven Mark 4/350°F/180°C for 15–20 minutes.

Reputation Maker

The Duchess of Bedford's Avocado Starter

Ingredients

1 ripe avocado
1 chopped hardboiled egg
½ peeled, finely chopped onion
2 peeled, chopped tomatoes
½ cup mayonnaise
paprika
dash vinegar
salt and pepper
1 shredded lettuce

Method

1 Scoop out and mash avocado.
2 Mix with the tomatoes, egg, onion, mayonnaise, seasonings and vinegar.
3 Serve in individual dishes on a bed of lettuce.

Should be served quickly after making, before it discolours.

May

ARIES

Venus and your own ruling planet Mars will be in Aries throughout the whole of May, so you ought to be in an unusually energetic and ebullient mood, and because both these planets make beautiful aspects to Saturn in your angle of romance, someone is bound to give you the kind of love and appreciation that has so far eluded you in 1977. Financially, however, the picture is rather gloomy. Mercury continues to be in retrograde motion until the 14th and it would be very unwise indeed to enter into new agreements or pin your faith on promises prior to this date. The dynamic and unpredictable planet Uranus in Scorpio now influences business relationships and partnership money matters and therefore you may well be forced into a position where a complete break or separation is the only solution.

TAURUS

Both the Sun and Mercury in Taurus are at an adverse angle to Saturn in Leo this May and developments which directly affect your home and family life could give you a lot of sleepless nights. Mercury in retrograde motion until the 14th means no one is going to give you direct or honest answers and you must ensure that you are not being deceived or hopelessly misled. Partnerships and very close personal relationships are a problem for Taurians at the moment because Uranus in your opposite sign of Scorpio indicates that although you have reached some kind of crossroads or turning point, the way ahead is insufficiently marked. The golden rule is when in doubt, do nothing, and, more important still, say only what is actually necessary. Let others exaggerate and promise the earth while you retain a true sense of perspective.

GEMINI

Each year, until the Sun enters your own birthsign around May 22, you have neither your customary amount of energy nor the ability to gauge how others will act or react. However, with Jupiter currently in your own birthsign you probably couldn't care less if others fail to respond. The world is very much your oyster now and it is your turn to prove that you are endowed with creative and artistic abilities which you are determined to use to the full. Do not, however, ignore minor health problems this month or believe that you can cope with pressures and problems totally alone. The Gemini mind is an agile one and you flit happily from subject to subject but Saturn in Leo is teaching you to become more of a perfectionist and it is better to be an authority on one subject than to dazzle others with your superficial knowledge.

CANCER

Emotionally, May is going to be a difficult and demanding month because until the 22nd the Sun in Taurus and opposing Uranus emphasizes what is wrong with relationships and makes you aware that it is time to cut yourself off completely from the past and start afresh, even though Cancerians are loth to let go or admit failure. Professionally, however, you will have a great deal going for you. Venus and Mars in Aries bring you in touch with people who can and will give you the opportunity to enhance your reputation and achieve your ambitions, and because both these planets make the best possible aspect to Saturn in Leo your financial security is assured if you are prepared to forget about insecurities and deficiencies and strike a hard bargain. There are certain times and phases in your life when you have the upper hand.

LEO

You have now to decide not only what it is you really want to achieve but also where you want to be. You may not have to be told that Saturn, currently in Leo, is forcing you to face up to reality and stop pretending that relationships and close involvements are without their flaws. You should, however, be more self-assured and self-sufficient now, realizing that if things have to be changed you have the ability and capacity to change them for the better. Career and professional interests are accentuated, but while Mercury is in retrograde motion until May 14 facts and information presented to you will not be the complete truth. Leo is a Fire sign, which means you are one of the world's doers, but you must admit you are too inclined to act on impulse and need always to curb your impatience.

VIRGO

Not all Virgos are cool characters, emotionally dispassionate and antiseptic, and you will have many opportunities this month to prove just how sentimental, sensitive – not to mention how outrageous – you can be. Maybe you have been kept in purdah too long and the time is right for you to have some fun. With both the Sun and your ruler Mercury in your angle of long-distance travel, obviously the place to let your hair down will be on a foreign shore, so it does not really matter how extrovert and wayward you become. Finances of course are a problem but it is more than likely that you have sufficient funds stashed away to enable you to pay for your pleasures. Jupiter is now passing through the midheaven or zenith of your solar horoscope.

LIBRA

Now it's your turn to be appreciated, wanted and adored – just the way you think you should be. Pluto in Libra for a very long time now has probably made you insecure and yearning for those moments when you are considered to be attractive, alluring and altogether desirable. What happened? Well, to begin with you probably devoted too much time and attention to achieving professional success and in the process alienated those who cared emotionally. Jupiter now in Gemini suggests that it really is time to pick yourself up, dust yourself off and start all over again, but this time make sure it's for real. Mars together with your own ruler Venus transits your opposite sign of Aries for the whole of May and if ever there was a time when you could make partnerships work, this is it.

SCORPIO

All the evil and nasty things that are said about this sign are not, in fact, true. What is certain is that Scorpio individuals never make a neutral impression. People either adore you or loathe you. Perhaps it is because the sign has rulership over the eighth house of the horoscope – the House of Death – that you are feared so much, and one seldom hears or reads a single word in praise of Scorpio's virtues. The basic quality of Scorpians is that you are a law unto yourselves; irrespective of the opinions of others, you alone choose your partners, your companions and occupations, etc., and power and determination are keynotes of your personalities. Until the 22nd you may just be in a mood to prove to partners and loved ones that the time has come to get things straight.

SAGITTARIUS

Sagittarius – the Archer. The planetary power or ruler associated with your sign is Jupiter, and as Jove is cheerful, optimistic, honourable, enterprising and very active, you should be super to live with. However, this is a contradictory sign, and in many ways similar to your opposite, Gemini – and we all know how changeable Geminians can be. Jupiter has now taken up a position in Gemini which means, for the time being, your luck is out. True, you should be able to achieve a considerable amount of headway at work this month, but you should not for one moment expect May to be a month of matrimonial bliss. In fact, if you anticipate partners being moody, malicious and merciless, you are not far off the mark.

CAPRICORN

Capricorns are frequently thought of as cantankerous and carping individuals, and maybe now that your own ruling planet Saturn is passing through your angle of joint finance and business interests you have a lot to complain about, but you are also expected to devote more time to the family, loved ones and very close relationships. Until May 14, however, Mercury will be in retrograde motion and a great deal that is said or implied will cut you to the quick. As you know, the Goat cannot be hurried or hustled, but this is one instance where you ought to take a leap into the dark and rely on the heart rather than the intellect. You have enormous reserves of energy and staying power but what you lack is flair, imagination and, occasionally, optimism.

AQUARIUS

If you did not take a greater interest in what was going on close to home last month, then you can only blame yourself if you are beset by domestic difficulties this May. Both the Sun and Mercury in Taurus are adversely aspected by baleful Saturn and the dynamic Uranus and you are bound to be hauled over the coals. True, you get a great deal of support from Jupiter and Pluto, but insufficient to allow you to presume that others will accept your ideas and opinions without a great deal of argument. A challenging month and perhaps one of the most decisive of the year for highly emotional and personal interests. Uranus will stay in Scorpio for a very long time yet to come and therefore it is difficult to predict what career or professional changes lie in store, but you would be right in thinking that some kind of change is inevitable.

PISCES

A great deal depends on your approach, methods and tactics this month and your ability to rationalize situations. A series of difficult aspects seem to indicate it is time to take a more practical view of both career and financial problems. There seems to be an area within the Pisces make-up which prevents you from using your many talents and abilities to the full and allows others to achieve the recognition that is rightfully yours. The planetary set-up is not a particularly pretty one but this does not mean you can't win or succeed – you can, but you must avoid getting too carried away by dreams and fantasies and it would be to your advantage to make a complete domestic or environmental change.

Monday
2

Bank Holiday in Scotland.
Booking opens for Edinburgh Festival.
Grand gathering of the Clans in Edinburgh.

Tuesday
3

Wednesday
4

Cricket County Championships start.

Thursday
5

Friday
6

Saturday
7

Sunday
8

Anniversary of VE Day. End of World War II against
Germany. Officially declared 32 years ago today.

Supertip
Make your own funnel from the
top of a plastic detergent bottle.
Cut through it 3 or 4 inches from
the top; turn it upside down to
form funnel.

Motherlore
Queen Charlotte's Ball at
Grosvenor House tonight.
Marks unofficial opening of
London Season. Not so many
debs around now to make their
curtsies, but there'll still be a few
dressed in white. The Ball is
modelled on Queen Charlotte's
birthday parties, at which all her
Maids of Honour were dressed in
white. Now it's all in a good
cause raising money for Queen
Charlotte's and Chelsea
Hospitals.

Supertip
Plastics don't conduct electricity
but they do build up static. They
attract and hold dust particles
like a magnet, and dust is dirt.
Which is why plastic gets grubby
so quickly. To stop plastics being
so attractive to dust, you can
smear them sparingly with liquid
detergent, then rinse off and dry.
Incidentally, as friction generates
static electricity, the more you
brush your man-made carpet, the
more it will attract the dust. (I
haven't heard such a good
argument against housework
since the marriage guidance
counsellor told me that the more
houseproud a woman is, the less
likely she is to be interested in
sex.) Anyway, to get back to the
carpet, shampooing with a
detergent will help to reduce
static.

Family Favourite

Watercress Soup

Ingredients
2 bunches watercress
½ oz/15 g butter
1½ pints/scant litre chicken stock
2 tablespoons flour
¼ pint/1½ dl milk
3 tablespoons cream
salt and pepper

Method
1 Wash watercress and remove any coarse stalks. Put aside one or two sprigs for garnish.
2 Gently cook the rest of the watercress in the butter for 3–4 minutes, add stock and seasoning, cover and simmer until soft (about 20 minutes).
3 Put through blender or sieve and return to saucepan.
4 Mix milk and flour to a thick cream, stir in a little of the watercress purée and return mixture to pan.
5 Bring to boil, stirring until it thickens, cook for further 3–4 minutes, and test for seasoning.
6 Stir in cream just before serving and garnish with sprigs of watercress.

Gardening

May Gardener

Sow runner beans, building a cane bean frame for them to climb, or choose dwarf French beans, which need no support.

Sow seeds of winter cabbage and winter cauliflower in a cosy little corner of the garden, for transplanting later. Plant out the seedling cauliflowers, Brussels sprouts, cabbage and leeks you have raised in boxes or beds. If you don't want the trouble of raising them yourself, buy the young plants.

Keep the weeds down by hoeing.

Deal ruthlessly with slugs and snails as they do enormous damage to young plants.

MAY

Monday
9

Lilac Time. Bluebells are coming out.
Good time for Kew.

Tuesday
10

Wednesday
11

Thursday
12

Friday
13

Saturday
14

Sunday
15

Motherlore
Whenever you're in a hurry,
force yourself to do things
SLOWER.

Supertip
Use Milton (the sterilizing liquid
used to clean babies' bottles) to
get rid of tea and coffee stains on
Melamine cups.

Supertip
When boiling rice, if you add 2
tablespoons cooking oil to the
water it won't boil over.

Slug traps
1 An inverted half of grapefruit
skin will trap slugs if you
place slug pellets underneath.
2 Put a small tin in a hole level
with the ground, half full of
milk and a little water. Slugs
will crawl in and drown.

Supertip
Plastic bathroom and shower
curtains will stay softer longer
(and last longer) if you add a few
drops of mineral oil to the warm
water of the final rinse when you
wash them.

Family Favourite

Kidneys in Sherry Sauce
Ingredients

12 lamb's kidneys
1 large onion, peeled and chopped
1 clove garlic, peeled and crushed
2 oz/50 g butter
1 oz/25 g flour
10 tablespoons dry sherry
$\frac{1}{4}$ pint/$1\frac{1}{2}$ dl water
1 beef bouillon cube
bayleaf
salt and pepper
handful of chopped parsley

Method

1 Remove skin and fat from kidneys, cut in half and remove cores.
2 Melt 1 oz/25 g of butter in a heavy pan, and gently fry onion until soft.
3 Add kidneys and cook for 3 minutes on each side until firm and slightly browned. Remove kidneys and onions and keep hot.
4 Melt remaining butter in pan, stir in flour and add garlic, stock cube water and sherry, stirring until smooth.
5 Add bayleaf and seasoning, bring sauce to the boil stirring all the time, then simmer until sauce thickens.
6 Add kidneys and onions to pan, cover and simmer for 5–10 minutes, or until kidneys are cooked.
7 Remove bayleaf, adjust seasoning, turn on to serving dish and garnish with parsley.

Family Favourite

Lady Ayer's Fried Cheese Sandwiches
Ingredients (For 1 sandwich)

2 buttered slices of bread
1 slice of cheese, the same size as the bread slices
1 slice ham (optional)
butter or olive oil

Method

1 Make a cheese sandwich, but butter *each side* of the bread.
2 Press the sandwich together and fry in hot butter or olive oil until golden brown on both sides.
3 Remove from pan and drain on kitchen paper.

To make a Croque Monsieur, include a slice of ham in the sandwich. Children love them.

Monday
16

Tuesday
17

Chelsea Flower Show opens (to May 20).

Wednesday
18

Thursday
19

Ascension Day or 'Holy Thursday'. The anniversary of
Christ's ascent into heaven, 40 days after Easter Sunday.

Friday
20

Sabotage television. It's Cup Final day tomorrow.

Saturday
21

Football Association Cup Final. Avoid Piccadilly Circus.

Sunday
22

'Beating the Parish Bounds'
ceremonies for the next three
days. Only a few churches still
continue these medieval
processions around the parish
boundaries dating from the time
when there were no written
maps. The vicar, churchwarden
and some of the choirboys go
round the parish and even
'bump' the youngest choirboy at
boundary points. The
processions always took place on
the three days preceding
Ascension Day.

Cleaning copper
Old and badly stained copper
should be immersed for a few
minutes only in a solution of
Harpic in water. When the
copper begins to change colour,
remove it and rinse thoroughly.
Finish polishing in the usual
way.

Supertip
It is often worthwhile, if you
want cheap meat, to remember
how the rule of supply and
demand operates at the butchers.
The cheapest cuts are not
necessarily the cheapest in poor
areas, where they are greatly in
demand, but in the more
affluent neighbourhoods where
most of the butcher's customers
don't even ask for them, he may
therefore slash the price to get
rid of them. So it may be worth a
short journey to buy expensive
meat in poor areas and cheap
meat in expensive areas.

Family Favourite

Quiche Lorraine

If you have unexpected guests, don't offer bacon and eggs. Whip up a quick quiche instead.

Ingredients

6 oz/175 g shortcrust pastry
1 small onion, peeled and finely chopped
4–6 rashers streaky bacon, with rind removed
2 eggs
2 oz/50 g grated cheese
¼ pint/1½ dl milk
1 tomato (optional)
salt and pepper

Method

1 Roll out pastry and line an 8-inch (21-cm) round flan ring. Trim edges, prick base well and bake at Mark 4/350°F/180°C for 10 minutes.
2 Fry onion gently until transparent, add chopped bacon and fry.
3 Remove from pan and drain and turn into pastry case.
4 Beat eggs with milk, cheese, season to taste and pour into flan.
5 Garnish with sliced tomato.
6 Bake at Mark 4/350°F/180°C for about 30 minutes until golden brown and set.

Reputation Maker

May Wine (Serves 30)

Ingredients

10 bottles dry cheap white wine (if possible Liebfraumilch, which smells of flowers anyway)
2 bottles brandy
1 lemon, sliced
1 orange, sliced
handful frozen strawberries
1 glass sherry
3 little muslin bags of dry woodruff (get it from Culpeper. If you're giving a party it's definitely worth the effort because it adds an unmistakable dry, nutty aroma)
3 handfuls May blossom
3 sprigs fresh lavender
3 sprigs fresh rosemary

Method

1 Put one bottle of wine into punch bowl, add strawberries, sherry, lemon and orange.
2 Add woodruff, then the other ingredients, ending with May blossom.
3 Chill and serve.

MAY

Monday
23

Tuesday
24

Wednesday
25

Thursday
26

Coal should be cheaper, if you stock up now at summer prices.

Friday
27

Saturday
28

Prepare for Open Air Concerts in the park.
Fashion Tip: check raincoat; buy large coloured umbrella.

Sunday
29

Whit Sunday or Pentecost. The festival to celebrate the descent of the Holy Ghost to visit the Apostles.

Supertip
No need to iron nylon or terylene curtains if you wash them this way: Fold them up neatly and soak first, then wash, keeping the articles still folded. Don't crumple. Rinse in the same way and drip dry.

Supertip
To avoid blisters on holiday, charity walks and the like, treat the feet at least a week previously by rubbing night and morning with surgical spirit.

Supertip
If a blanket or bedcover is too short, sew a wide strip of material to the bottom which can then be tucked in and not seen. Similar strips can be sewn to the sides of an eiderdown.

May Cook
Spring-clean deep freeze. Trout, salmon and asparagus coming up for summer treats.

Supertip
When serving anything frozen *add something fresh*. A pinch of grated lemon peel, a dollop of cream, a slosh of wine, coarsely ground black pepper, a bit of butter, a grating of nutmeg on home-frozen mashed potato or shop-frozen spinach.

Reputation Maker

Clement Freud's Chicken Mousse
(Good for using up leftover weekend chicken)

Ingredients

2 oz/50 g butter
3 oz/75 g white breadcrumbs
¼ pint/1½ dl single cream
8 oz/225 g chopped chicken meat
3 eggs
3 tablespoons dry sherry
salt
nutmeg

This is delicious served with a creamy, slightly garlic mayonnaise, to which you add a chopped avocado pear.

Method

1 Melt butter in a basin over a pan of boiling water.
2 Add breadcrumbs, cream, salt and a good pinch of nutmeg and stir for about 5 minutes, as the mixture thickens.
3 Add eggs and sherry, well beaten together, and finally put in the chopped chicken.
4 Pour mixture into a buttered mould or soufflé dish, cover with foil and cook in a Mark 4/350°F/180°C oven until firm, which should take about 30 minutes.
5 Leave to cool and serve chilled.

Family Favourite

French Bean Salad

Ingredients

1 lb/450 g French beans
2 tablespoons French dressing

Method

1 Trim and slice some French beans rather coarsely and cook them in plenty of boiling water, until just tender but still crunchy.
2 Drain.
3 While still warm, toss in French dressing. Serve cold. Good with fried fish or grilled meat.

June

ARIES

Oh dear, another dreary month financially. However, with your own ruler Mars in Taurus opposing the unremitting Uranus in Scorpio, you really can't expect it to be otherwise. You could of course admit you have been extravagant and imprudent but excuses won't placate the bank manager or your creditors. This said, there are some reassuring aspects in June; to begin with, Jupiter is close to the Sun on the 4th and relatives will be less inclined to castigate and carp, while Saturn strongly placed in Leo means your emotional security is not in jeopardy. Planets are especially potent in certain signs and you are continually being harassed by Pluto in Libra, seemingly intent on making you aware of the meaning of the word 'partnership' – the legal and moral contract which binds two people together.

TAURUS

Now both Mars and your own ruler Venus will be in Taurus – at an adverse angle to Saturn in Leo – so there is no escape from family and domestic dramas. Emerson wrote that 'Astrology is astronomy brought to earth and applied to the affairs of men.' What he did not tell us was how someone born under the influence of gentle Venus copes with persistent pettiness in partners or petulant relatives. But cope you must, perhaps by being less concerned with the materialistic and more interested in the spiritual. However, Taurus is an Earth sign and you must have your creature comforts. Throughout June the Sun and Jupiter relate well to Pluto, indicative that at least things will be going well for you at work and that at least your artistic or creative talents will be appreciated.

GEMINI

Surely the fellow who said ' 'Tis always morning somewhere in the world' must have been born under Gemini. You really do prefer to believe it's always darkest before the dawn, and of course you are right. Jupiter currently in Gemini should in fact be making you more optimistic, good-natured and philosophical than ever. However, don't over-extend yourself while there are some adverse aspects to Saturn and Uranus this month. Problems you thought long since resolved are likely to re-emerge and you may have to admit you have been a little too over-confident too soon. It is going to be a difficult month for work and career issues and either you will find your own energies rather depleted or a member of the family will require medical attention. In any event, take no chances.

CANCER

You have a complex planetary set-up to contend with this month. The Sun in Gemini until the 22nd, when it enters your own birthsign, tends to exert a debilitating influence and no one gives you completely direct answers. Finances of course are a bore with dreary old Saturn making you pay heavily for your pleasures and proving there is no escape from obligations and commitments. However, what is nice now is that you will be forming new friendships and attachments, some of which could really take your heart on a joy-ride – an excursion you will be only too willing to experience. As you may know, Cancer is ruled by the Moon and is supposedly the most feminine sign of the Zodiac, It has been said – somewhat poetically – that the Moon in all its varying stages is constant in its inconstancy.

LEO

It would be nice to be able to tell you that you are going to get a lot of sympathy, understanding and affection but a series of wretched aspects to Saturn in your own birthsign indicate the truth will be otherwise. Why does everyone expect Leos to be jolly, confident and the people who get things done? Surely you are allowed to feel inadequate and insecure sometimes? Well, you can try playing the helpless waif or the martyr but the chances are you still have to take the decisions, raise the cash, do the arranging and feed the cat. But there must be some joy in this dreary month of June. There is – one planet, Neptune in Sagittarius, relates well to Saturn and an old romance or attachment could well be rekindled. That is of course if you can forgive them sufficiently to give them a second chance – what was it they did, or didn't do, anyway?

VIRGO

It would help a lot if you wore a happy face this month. There will be far too many depressing ones around. What have you got to be jolly about? Well, you weren't born under Leo for one thing – or even worse at the moment, Aquarius, not to mention Taurus and Scorpio, two more signs currently afflicted by Saturn. Plus the fact that you will have a lot going for you even if it means taking off for foreign parts to find romance and appreciation. And the aspects relating to finances are not at all bad – not sensational, but better than they have been for a considerable time past. Jupiter in Gemini should bring you in touch with people who can and will further your aims. Virgos pretend not to be ambitious.

LIBRA

You should know by now that friendships and finances just do not mix and you will probably be scratching around to pay your way this June while people who should repay their debts seem oblivious to your dilemma. It is believed that a need for beauty and artistic expression is an essential facet of the Libran make-up and if people born under this sign do not find the satisfaction in life they seek, they become escapists, inventing a fantasy world of their own. You hate anything sordid; you may accept poverty, never squalor. Poverty you may have to endure a little longer, but with Jupiter currently in Gemini making the best possible aspect to Pluto in Libra, there should be more than a glimmer of light at the end of the tunnel. June is a month to travel, not only to find the perfect place to relax and unwind but also to establish business contacts which will be useful late in the year.

SCORPIO

Mars enters your opposite sign of Taurus on June 7 and stays there until the middle of July, so this can be a rather turbulent period in the matrimonial and partnership stakes. Careerwise also you are not exactly in a strong enough position to dictate terms or even cajole superiors into submission. Saturn in Leo is adversely aspected, meaning – cool it for a while, re-think, re-plan and reorganize. However, the relationship between Jupiter and your own ruler Pluto is a favourable one and situations which develop in an indirect or roundabout way improve partnership finances. Most Scorpios are gifted with second sight and you have an alarming capacity for uncovering secrets.

SAGITTARIUS

Why do the wrong people travel and the right people stay back home? Wherever you go this month you are not likely to discover the solace and solitude for which you yearn. Come to think of it, June is seldom one of your better months, but that's because until the 21st the Sun is passing through your opposite sign of Gemini and you find others, and partners in particular, unimaginative, unco-operative and a trifle dull. Now with Jupiter, your own ruler, also in Gemini, you have neither the energy nor the desire to argue. Not a very cheery prospect, is it? But then all the signs of the Zodiac are having a rough time because there are a lot of conflicts between the major planets, so try to display that characteristic attributed to your birthsign – optimism.

CAPRICORN

In spite of work going well, in fact, fabulously well, this won't be a very good month for money. Joint finances and business interests are now dominated by your own rather baleful planet Saturn and a few nasty aspects from both Mars and Uranus this June could leave partners in a frightful tizzy. However, you have a reputation for being totally realistic and capable of an enormous amount of fortitude, so again you are expected to steer the ship into calmer waters and do the repair job. But, as if in a way to compensate for all the dreariness, Venus and Mars in Taurus after June 7 add some sparkle and more excitement to emotional involvements and make you feel less hard done by. Many Capricorns are late developers and seem to come into their own after the bloom of youth has flown.

AQUARIUS

Let everyone know that with Saturn now passing through Leo, the seventh house of your solar horoscope, you can't be expected to be either the party person or the one who resolves everybody else's personal problems. You have enough matrimonial, partnership and domestic ones of your own to cope with. But cope with them you will and must because there is no escape. However, with both the Sun and Jupiter in Gemini this June you will begin to realize that what is needed is a more tactful and sensitive approach rather than insisting that others accept your brand of logic or your idea of the way things should be done. It is difficult for you as an Aquarian to admit that you can be obstinate, intolerant and over-sensitive because you like to be thought of as moderate and reasonable.

PISCES

You should be that much more sure of where you are at and where you are going this month. And, perhaps more important still, for the ever-romantic Piscean, who's going to be your travelling companion. However, before you can take off in any direction you must resolve work and career problems once and for all. Not an easy task to set yourself but an unavoidable one now that Saturn in Leo is forcing you to stop deliberating and procrastinating and realize that you can't rely on others for support or assistance. When the Sun enters the sign of Cancer on June 22 you will know that you can make it alone, also that success will come in a totally new environment and maybe even a foreign country. June, therefore, will at times be exasperating and demanding.

Monday
30

Tuesday
31

Glyndebourne Festival Opera opens (to August 6).
Music and elegant picnics, with grazing sheep off-stage.

Wednesday

Cast clout. Open season for brides.
Invitations going out for Buckingham Palace Garden Parties.
Derby Day at Epsom.

Thursday

The Oaks – the Fillies Classic race at Epsom.

Friday

Bath Festival (to June 12). Look in at Longleat on the way.
Book up at Popjoys Restaurant for dinner.
Check food supplies – holidays until next Wednesday.

Saturday
4

Sunday

Trinity Sunday. Festival in honour of the Trinity, chosen for
today by Thomas à Becket in the 12th century.

Supertip
There's a long Bank Holiday
weekend coming up, so start
planning menus.

Supertip
Almost any fresh fruit, from
oranges to grapes, tastes
delicious when peeled, chopped,
sprinkled with a little white wine
and optional sugar and then
served in individual wineglasses
(any old shape or size) with an
optional dab of fresh or sugar-
sprinkled sour cream.

Motherlore
When planning the first summer
picnic remember that butter
melts, mayonnaise curdles and
jars and bottles leak.

Popjoys Restaurant
(telephone Bath (0225) 60494)

Supertip
When drying sheets fold them
into four while still wet and peg
with three pegs to the line. This
way the material will not drop
out of shape and will be much
easier to iron.

Gardening

June Gardener

Real growing things (peas and beans) start to appear. Intense excitement! Continue hoeing with added impetus.

Last chance to sow peas and beans from seed for second crop in September. Sow lettuce, chicory, radishes, turnips from seeds.

Young home-grown vegetables, peas, beans, etc. all plentiful, but should be cheaper later.

Beginning of summer brings abundance of fruit. Buy or gather strawberries, raspberries, loganberries, etc. for jam or freezing.

Fresh herbs ready for drying or freezing – mint, chives, chervil, etc.

You're supposed to make your Christmas puddings, but hopefully you're lazing in the garden and probably won't feel in the mood until November, when I have an idea up my sleeve for you.

Reputation Maker

Princess Margaret's Avocado Pear Soup

Ingredients

3–4 avocado pears (depending on size)
1 pint/6 dl chicken consommé
½ teaspoon pepper
pinch garlic salt
1 teaspoon Worcester sauce
1 dessertspoon horseradish sauce
a little dry sherry
double cream
pinch of salt and pinch of sugar

Method

1 Scoop out avocado pulp, discard skin and put all ingredients except cream in a blender or through a mill.
2 After blending leave in refrigerator for 1 hour.
3 Serve with a dab of double cream on top of each portion.

Reputation Maker

Greek Yoghurt Salad (Tsatsiki)

Ingredients

½ pint/3 dl yoghurt
½ cucumber, peeled and diced; a few thin slices to garnish
1 peeled and crushed clove garlic, or coarsely chopped mint leaves

Method

Stir all ingredients with salt and pepper into the yoghurt and serve very cold, garnished.

JUNE

Monday
 6

Spring Bank Holiday.

With any luck picnic season starts; straw hats and punts, strawberries and cream, roses, fresh peas, and cucumber sandwiches.

Tuesday
 7

Bank Holiday to celebrate Queen's Silver Jubilee.
H.M. and Prince Philip drive through London in state for Thanksgiving Ceremony at St Paul's Cathedral.

Wednesday
 8

Grosvenor House Antiques Fair opens in London. Very expensive.

Supertip
If you have unusually flat feet, want to wear high-heeled boots and find they have no arch support, buy a heel pillow and stick this in upside down, i.e. heel part facing the toe end. This provides ample arch support for the flattest foot.

Thursday
 9

Motherlore
What June brides need is a non-stick, easy to clean, crack, chip, scratch and smash proof, stackable, comprehensive set of inexpensive pots that will stand up to the hot plate, oven and deep freeze and be smart enough to end up on the dining room table.

Friday
 10

Saturday
 11

Commonwealth Day.
The Queen's official birthday. Royal family get together for Trooping the Colour.

Sunday
12

Motherlore
'A robust love of life is what attracts a man more than beauty,' said Anita Loos, who wrote *Gentlemen Prefer Blondes*.

Family Favourite

Soufflé Omelette

Ingredients
8 eggs
salt and pepper
butter

Optional – after folding in yolks add a cup of peeled prawns.

Method
1 Grease inside of the frying pan, including the edge.
2 Separate yolks and whites of eggs. Whisk yolks lightly, adding salt and pepper.
3 Whisk egg whites until stiff and peaky, then fold in yolks.
4 Put pan over a good heat, add egg and cook without touching it, until the edge of the omelette comes easily away from the edge of the pan.
5 Put pan under a hot grill and cook until top of the omelette has risen and set.

Reputation Maker

Summer Punch (Serves 24)

Ingredients
1 bottle dry red wine
2 bottles sparkling white wine
½ bottle brandy
½ lb/225 g raspberries, fresh or frozen
2 pints/1½ litres soda water
2 tablespoonfuls sugar

Method
1 Put lots of ice into a large bowl.
2 Pour the red wine and brandy over ice, sprinkle on the sugar and stir well.
3 Add raspberries and leave to stand in a cold place for an hour.
4 Just before serving pour in the soda water and sparkling white wine.

JUNE

Monday
13

Tuesday
14

Royal Ascot Week begins. What will Mrs Shilling show us?

Wednesday
15

Thursday
16

Overhaul television. Wimbledon tennis starts on Monday.
Anglers out. Freshwater coarse fishing season starts.
First Test Match at Lord's. England plays the Australians.

Friday
17

Saturday
18

Waterloo Day (1815)—we beat the French.

Sunday
19

Father's Day. No sage socks. No pipe. No copy of *Penthouse*.
Serve Steak and Kidney Pie again.

Supertip
Fry pork chops with some thin
slices of apple.

Supertip
To scrape new potatoes, put in a
bowl and cover with boiling
water for 2 minutes; then the
skins come off easily.

Way to clean spotty ties
Soak a piece of cotton wool in
surgical spirit and rub gently on
spot mark. Then run cotton
wool over the whole of the tie
so you're not left with a
watermark. Dries very
quickly. No smell left. No
pressing problem. Particularly
good for grease marks.

Supertip
If you lose your front door key
ask the police to recommend a
locksmith and help you get the
door open.

Family Favourite

Cheese Tart

Delicious hot or cold.

Ingredients

shortcrust pastry for 8-inch (21-cm) flan
   tin
2 eggs
4 oz/100 g grated Gruyère cheese
pinch of nutmeg
salt and pepper
$\frac{1}{4}$ pint/$1\frac{1}{2}$ dl double cream
$\frac{1}{4}$ pint/$1\frac{1}{2}$ dl milk

Method

1 Line flan tin with pastry, prick well
   and bake at Mark 4/350°F/180°C for
   10 minutes.
2 Beat eggs, add cheese.
3 Season well, add milk and cream.
4 Stir well together and pour into pastry
   case.
5 Bake at Mark 4/350°F/180°C for 30
   minutes.

Reputation Maker

Elderflower Champagne

Ingredients

3 heads of elderflower
$1\frac{1}{2}$ lb/675 g white sugar
juice and rind of 1 lemon
2 tablespoons white vinegar
1 gallon/$4\frac{1}{2}$ litres cold water

4 screw-top bottles (such as cider or soft
   drink bottles, which are designed to
   take fizzy drinks)

Method

1 Put sugar and water into washing-up
   bowl and stir until sugar has dissolved.
2 Add remaining ingredients; leave to
   stand for 24 hours.
3 Strain into bottles and leave in a cool
   place for 2 weeks before drinking.

When I first made this I never expected
it to taste like champagne. But it did.
Sweet, fizzy, cheap Spanish champagne.
But it's fun to make and has a unique,
delicate flowery fragrance.
Chill well before serving.

JUNE

Monday
20

Wimbledon Championships start today.
It's the 100th Anniversary of the Championships.
Lots of Centenary celebrations planned.

Tuesday
21

Summer solstice. Avoid Stonehenge – full of Druids.
Royal Highland Show opens.

Motherlore
The day when the sun enters
the sign of Cancer and reaches
its most northerly distance
from the equator. Gives us the
longest day and shortest night
of the year.

Wednesday
22

Thursday
23

Nice night for a Midsummer-eve party.

Motherlore
The night you try two
traditional rituals for finding out
who your true love will be.
1 Sit alone in front of a mirror
   by candlelight and you will
   see your true love behind you.
   Or,
2 Take an apple, remove the
   peel in one piece. Swing it
   round your head and let it go
   on the third time around so it
   lands on the floor behind you.
   You should find it spells out
   the initials of Lord Right.

Friday
24

Midsummer Day (Quarter Day).

Saturday
25

Sunday
26

United Nations Charter signed in San Francisco (1945).

Family Favourite

Swift Salad Soup

Ingredients
1 chicken bouillon cube
1 tablespoon double cream
2 peeled tomatoes
½ cucumber
1 heart lettuce
scrap of crushed garlic
1 pint/6 dl milk

Method
1 Finely chop all salad ingredients.
2 Melt bouillon cube in 4 tablespoons boiling water, with garlic.
3 Add remaining ingredients and chill before serving.

These quantities are a rough guide. Use whatever salad vegetables you have around. You might double up on the lettuce and cut out the tomatoes, or include a bunch of watercress and eliminate the cucumber.

Reputation Maker

3 Sauces to Serve with Vanilla, Coffee or Chocolate Ice Cream

1 Minted Chocolate Sauce

Ingredients
10 large chocolate mints
3 tablespoons single cream

Method
1 Melt chocolate mints in a bowl over boiling water.
2 Stir in cream; serve hot or cold.

2 Hot Fudge Sauce

Ingredients
2 Mars bars
4 tablespoons milk

Method
1 Slice Mars bars into a basin.
2 Put basin over pan of boiling water and melt bars in 4 tablespoons of hot milk, stirring constantly. Serve hot.

3 Rum Chocolate Sauce

Ingredients
¼ lb/100 g semi-sweet chocolate
¼ pint/1½ dl double cream
1 tablespoon rum (or Grand Marnier or cognac)

Method
1 Melt chocolate in a bowl over a pan of boiling water.
2 Gradually stir in cream and heat through, but do not allow to boil.
3 Add cognac, rum or Grand Marnier. Serve hot.

July

ARIES

'Whither so fast? See how the kindly flowers perfume the air, and all to make thee stay.' Stay and rest awhile now; contemplate, ponder and re-cap and get your house in order. The Sun in Cancer until July 22 accentuates home and family affairs and you must concede that although as an Arian you do need a secure base from which to operate, you do not always appreciate the efforts others make to cosset you. In mythology, there was no way that Mars could be smothered by affection. Saturn currently in your angle of romance means you ought to be finding the right kind of affection now from a person who is strong enough to make you secure without stifling you – which must be nice. And, to make you really cheerful, after July 18 you won't be plagued with quite so many financial problems.

TAURUS

You will have to wait until Mars leaves your own birthsign on July 18 before you can find any real peace of mind or anything like permanent solutions to matrimonial and partnership problems. But this should be a month when you discover that the scales of justice are not so decidedly tipped against you and loved ones or lovers at least appreciate some of your virtues. Perhaps your greatest attribute is that you are steadfast – plodding and unbelievably stubborn at times, but steadfast nevertheless. There is an unusual amount of emphasis on finances this July. Jupiter, Venus and finally Mars all in Gemini should make it easier for you to ask for and get a rise or more housekeeping money and although Saturn continues to make you rather unsettled in your home, the pressures will be less intense.

GEMINI

There is so much planetary activity in your own birthsign this month that you are bound to feel rather elated and certainly in better shape physically. However, wait until Mars enters Gemini on the 19th before burning too many candles at both ends. For years now, Neptune in your opposite sign of Sagittarius has exerted a confusing and nebulous influence on matrimonial and partnership affairs and at times you must have wondered whether you have made the right choice. The answer is, in a word, yes, but you must accept the fact that others may not have sufficient command of words to express their deepest feelings and you must take a lot on trust. Saturn in Leo, however, is very probably making you more profound and if you persevere you may come up with some concepts of your own.

CANCER

July may not begin brilliantly because the Sun and Mercury in Cancer will be at an adverse aspect to Pluto and you will be playing that old Cancerian game of 'let's remember' rather than looking forward. There is nothing to be gained by a mournful contemplation of the ruins of the past, but only after someone gives you a tweak will you realize that. You have only yourself to blame if you are not invited to parties, picnics and balls. At the end of August, Jupiter enters your own birthsign, where it will remain until the end of the year. This only happens once every 12 years and when it does you know for sure that one man in your arms is better than a thousand in your dreams. Also it ensures that if you have been searching for that one man, you are certain to find him. Lucky you!

LEO

It was Noel Coward who said 'we know God made trees and the birds and the bees and the seas for the fishes to swim in. We're also aware that he had quite a flair for making exceptional women.' Surely he must have been talking about Leo ladies. He was, in fact, talking about a Capricorn – Marlene, no less. Born with the Sun as your ruler, you are in a way exceptional, and with Saturn currently passing through your own birthsign you are expected to prove it by being more resourceful, resilient and ready to discard all the flotsam accumulated in the misguided belief that it added to your security. Saturn remoulds, re-forms and re-shapes one's life for the better. It also makes one less concerned with material possessions and brings wisdom, erudition and a real sense of values.

VIRGO

July doesn't have to be depressing or dull. It opens with Mars and Venus in Taurus ensuring that your outlook, in spite of a number of personal doubts and inhibitions, should be a relatively positive and optimistic one, and with good reason. By mid-month, Jupiter sparkling away in the midheaven of your solar birth-chart is joined by these self-same planets and if ever there was a moment to prove that you have star quality, this is it. Not all Virgos are introspective, analytical sceptics – quite a few are noted for their outrageousness and sense of the ridiculous. What you do have is marvellous clarity and an eye for detail. Personal relationships are a bit of a problem at the moment but insufficient to prevent you from proving that you are not a second-class person.

LIBRA

Oscar Wilde could only have been a Libran – of course he was: 'In married life, three is company and two none.' You won't want to be encumbered with any permanent relationships this month. Three planets in your angle of long-distance travel all relate beautifully to Pluto in Libra and it is very much a case of off with the old and on with the new and to hell with finances! 1977 so far has probably been a bit of a let-down, and a Libran – more than anybody else – needs reassurance. Yours is the only sign symbolized by an inanimate object – the Scales; all the rest are either people, animals or creatures and, even with luscious Venus as your ruler, you are not as emotionally secure as others imagine. The time is quickly approaching when you enter the most crucial phase of the year for your career and profession.

SCORPIO

It's a bit miserable having Mars in your opposite sign of Taurus because it means partners, lovers – in fact, all those you care about – don't care very much about you. Fortunately, this unhappy state of affairs only continues until July 18, when Mars moves into Gemini, but even then you will be slightly at a disadvantage in any joint financial or business arrangement. Not to worry; with Uranus becoming a constructive rather than a destructive force in your own birthsign after July 17, you will be at your most creative, inventive and resilient and a match for anyone. There is some doubt as to which planet rules Scorpio. Until Pluto was discovered in the thirties Mars seemed to be the chap, but Pluto, the god of the Underworld and the unknown, is more akin to your nature.

SAGITTARIUS

If you want the blunt truth, read on. If you don't, continue to believe that the current conflicts in partnerships and close relationships are the fault of the other person, not yours. But with your own ruler Jupiter and Mars and Venus in your opposite sign this month the odds are definitely stacked against you. Mars, as you know, is the Warrior, and between July 19 and September 1 it is likely to be open warfare – but at least nothing is concealed and you know exactly where you stand. Sagittarians are considered to be happy-go-lucky and it is probably because you have taken too much for granted that you now find you are asked to state, honestly and directly, where your true feelings lie and what you are going to do to prove your emotions and devotions are for real.

CAPRICORN

Each year while the Sun is passing through your opposite sign of Cancer until July 22 you don't have your usual amount of energy and you are easily upset when partners play you up. However, the overall planetary picture this month is a dynamic one and if you are a typical Capricorn you'll grasp any and every opportunity to enhance both your personal and professional prestige. However, wait until Mars enters Gemini on July 18 before focusing your sights on the summit. Undoubtedly you'll get there. Mars, Jupiter and Venus, all beautifully aspected to Pluto in Libra, can't fail to bring you the kind of recognition you need and, truth to tell, deserve. But it's also a month to have a bit more fun and to make those around you see that you are not humourless, heavy and untouched by a show of emotion.

AQUARIUS

You'll get a great deal more sympathy this month if you don't ask for it. In fact, with a lot of planets well placed in your solar horoscope, you should really have no time for tears. Apart from boring old Saturn still forcing you to face up to the reality of partnership problems, the outlook is bright and more encouraging than it has been for many, many months past. Domestic dramas will definitely be on the decline after the 18th and with Jupiter, Mars and Venus all in your angle of romance, who knows – in the nick of time you may even discover true love isn't just the prerogative of the other eleven signs of the Zodiac. You are entitled to, and will get, your share. One day you'll realize that the heart of the matter is the matter of the heart.

PISCES

With all that's gone before, you may not be prepared to believe that throughout the remainder of 1977 you could just find the tranquillity and reassurance which you seek. True, you have a few turbulent weeks ahead and a lot of domestic difficulties to resolve, but once Jupiter enters Cancer in late August those two fishes will not be swimming in opposite directions any longer and emotionally you should be pulled together rather than being constantly pulled apart. But first the domestic drama bit – Mars in Gemini after July 18 means that if those with whom you share your home and domestic set-up want to battle and babble on about how much they do for you, then don't bother to argue; simply smile, genuflect and buy a one-way ticket to anywhere inaccessible.

Monday
27

Tuesday
28

Wednesday
29

Summer sales starting soon. Check linen and china cupboard replacement list. Look out for bargains.

Thursday
30

Henley Royal Regatta starts (to July 3).

Friday
1

Ladies' Finals and Men's doubles at Wimbledon.
Cheltenham International Festival of Music.

Saturday
2

Men's finals, Ladies' doubles and mixed doubles at Wimbledon.

Sunday
3

Dog Days begin (they end August 15). They are the days of great heat in the Northern Hemisphere, according to the Ancient Romans. The theory was that when the Dog Star rose with the Sun it added its heat to that of the celestial orb.

Frosted redcurrants and cherries

Hold the sprays of currants or little bunches of cherries by their stalks and dip first into beaten egg white and then into granulated sugar. Dry off in the fridge, chill until needed.

Motherlore

Don't listen to what he says, watch what he does . . .

Supertip

Book for central heating maintenance check. Don't wait until October or you'll never get a booking. For an annual charge of £15 (£17 in London), see if you can sign up for the Gas Board's Three Star scheme. The Board will remember to service your system and price includes insurance to cover costs of any parts that go wrong, so there's no more to pay and you're entitled to free emergency service.

Supertip

Potted plants water themselves when you are on holiday, if you stand them on foam rubber or a wet crumpled newspaper, in a bowl or bath containing a little water. (Bottom of pot must be above water level.)

Reputation Maker

Chicken Superwoman

(Invented by Trompetto, the Savoy chef de cuisine)

Ingredients

1 large chicken
1 tablespoon flour
2 oz/50 g butter
1 dessertspoon chopped shallots
4 fresh artichoke bottoms, cut into 4
   (or one 12-oz/350-g can of artichoke
   bottoms, *not* hearts)
1 glass dry white wine (4 oz/1½ dl)
2 lemons
¼ pint/1½ dl double cream
salt and pepper

Method

1 Divide chicken into 8 joints.
2 Put carcass, bones and giblets into a saucepan with seasoning and herbs to make stock.
3 Coat chicken joints in flour, fry in hot butter until golden brown.
4 Add shallots and artichoke bottoms, immediately pour on wine and bring to boil.
5 Now add about one-third pint chicken stock and juice of half a lemon.
6 Cover and cook until tender (about 40 minutes).
7 Grate zest off lemons.
8 When chicken is tender, pour cream over it and sprinkle in lemon zest.
9 Season to taste, adding more lemon juice if wanted.
10 Simmer gently for 5-6 minutes without lid until sauce is slightly reduced and of creamy texture.
11 Serve on its own, or with new potatoes or a few cooked noodles strained and shaken in butter.

Gardening

July Gardener

If you aren't on holiday, earth up potatoes ('earth up' means draw soil with a hoe around the potato stems).

Plant out winter cabbage and cauliflowers from seedbed.
Last chance to sow lettuce and radish seed.

JULY

Monday

Independence Day in the U.S.A. – Americans have a holiday to celebrate victory against the English colonials in 1776.

Supertip
Vinegar in rinsing water makes glasses shine.

Tuesday

Open air Tynwald Assembly, Isle of Man.
International Music Eisteddfod begins at Llangollen, Clwyd.
Brighton Festival (to July 17).

Open air Tynwald Assembly, Isle of Man, when all the Acts passed by the Manx Parliament are announced to the people. An historic Manx ceremony which has been held for over 1,000 years, since Norse times.

Wednesday

Thursday

Parliament breaks up soon. Write last letters to your MP before he goes off for the summer.
Second Test Match at Old Trafford.

Supertip
Paint electric light switches with phosphorescent paint so you can find them easily in the dark. Good for a child's room.

Friday

Supertip
Get seaweed or grass stains off clothes with methylated spirit.

Saturday

Sunday

Motherlore
If you're going to be late, take even more time and arrive even later, but looking calm and exquisite because that way you are more likely to be forgiven.

Reputation Maker

Seafood Salad

An exotic dish for people who live in big cities with good fish shops. Especially nutritious because there's no wasted protein, no bones and no fat. And it's my favourite food.

Ingredients
1 lb/450 g octopus
1 lb/450 g squid
4 oz/100 g shelled shrimps
1 handful chopped parsley
$\frac{1}{4}$ pint/1$\frac{1}{2}$ dl French dressing
a few unshelled prawns
and slices of cucumber } garnish

Method
1 Boil octopus and squid together for 20 minutes – not longer. Drain.
2 Cut octopus into bite-sized pieces.
3 Cut each squid in half and take out central 'plastic bag'. Throw away 'bag' and contents.
4 Chop squid into bite-sized pieces.
5 Mix octopus, squid, shrimps and parsley with French dressing.
6 Place on serving dish and decorate with prawns.

Family Favourite

Baked Eggs en Cocotte
Ingredients
4 tablespoons double cream
4 eggs
salt and pepper

Method
1 Butter 4 individual soufflé dishes or ovenproof ramekins.
2 Pour 1 tablespoon double cream into each dish.
3 Break an egg into the cream and add salt and pepper to taste.
4 Put a knob of butter on each egg.
5 Put the dishes in a pan of hot water and bake in a moderate oven Mark 4 / 350°F/180°C for about 15 minutes, or until whites are just set.

JULY

Monday
11

International T.T. Races, Isle of Man (that's motorbikes).
Royal International Horse Show opens at Wembley (until
Saturday).

Tuesday
12

Bank Holiday, Northern Ireland.

Wednesday
13

Thursday
14

France celebrates its National Day. Remember the Fall of
the Bastille in 1789.

Friday
15

St Swithin's Day.
Haslemere (Surrey) Festival opens (to May 23).
It's the second longest-running Festival in Britain.

Saturday
16

Sunday
17

Supertip
To remove chewing gum from
clothing scrape off as much as
possible with your fingernail.
Then soften the remainder with
white spirit and keep on
scraping. Test the material for
colour fastness first. Don't try to
wash it off because chewing gum
is waterproof.

Easy entertaining
Two dinner parties on two
consecutive nights are cheaper
than two spaced out – same
flowers, less cleaning and you
always buy too much anyway.
Even use the same meal and
precook it all at once.

Motherlore
Legend is if it rains today it'll
carry on for next 40 days. If
not, look forward to long dry
summer.

Supertip
Plastic cutlery trays – knife
boxes in fact – can also be used
to sort out your drawers for
jewellery, make-up, tiny
children's toys or medicine.

Supertip
The secret of saucepan-lid filing
is a length of curtain wire or
elastic across the back of a
cupboard – logically the
saucepan cupboard door – fixed
at intervals with drawing pins or
upholstery tacks. Tuck the lids
behind it.

Family Favourite

Barbecue Sauce (Serve with chops, sausages, hamburgers)

Ingredients
1 onion, finely chopped
1 oz/25 g butter
4 tablespoons vinegar·
2 level tablespoons brown sugar
6 level tablespoons tomato ketchup
1 tablespoon Worcester sauce
2 level teaspoons French mustard
celery salt (optional)
4 tablespoons water
½ level teaspoon salt
pepper

Method
1 Fry onion in melted butter until soft and golden brown.
2 Blend other ingredients, add to onion, stir well and reduce heat.
3 Simmer gently for 30 minutes, until sauce is slightly thickened.

Traditional Dish

Crême Brûlée
(In spite of its French name, a traditional Trinity College, Cambridge, dish)

Ingredients
1 pint/6 dl cream (¼ pint/1½ dl single, ¾ pint/4 dl double)
2 tablespoons caster sugar
5 egg yolks, beaten
4 tablespoons demerara sugar

Note: If you don't have a double boiler, heat the cream and caster sugar in a small saucepan, add the egg yolks and finish cooking in a mixing bowl, firmly wedged in the top of a saucepan of simmering water, but not touching water.

Method
1 Using the top pan of a double boiler, heat the cream and caster sugar over gentle flame and simmer for 1 minute, stirring continuously.
2 Remove from heat and add the beaten egg yolks, still stirring.
3 Place the top pan of the double boiler over the bottom half containing 1 inch of boiling water and cook for 5 minutes, stirring all the time.
4 Pour the crême into a shallow heat-proof dish or individual bowls.
5 Chill for at least one hour, then sprinkle top with the demerara sugar and grill gently until sugar melts.
6 Chill until needed, when the top will be a crackly toffee.

JULY

Monday
18

Supertip
If a biro dries up try holding it under the hot water tap for a few minutes.

Tuesday
19

Long school holidays are with us – or about to start.
Royal Welsh Agricultural Show opens at Builth Wells.

Motherlore
You're asking for trouble if you don't use a laundry or dry cleaner who isn't a member of the Association of British Launderers & Cleaners Ltd, Lancaster Gate House, 319 Pinner Road, Harrow, Middlesex. (Consult them for address of your nearest member.)

Wednesday
20

American astronauts became first men to land on the moon 8 years ago today.

Thursday
21

Friday
22

How to make Curds and Whey (little Miss Muffet's pudding)
Add $\frac{1}{2}$ teaspoon citric acid (from the chemist) to a wineglass of milk.

Saturday
23

Sunday
24

Old wive's cure for warts
Rub three or four times daily with a small piece of washing soda dipped in water. Continue this for weeks.

Reputation Maker

Never-fail Fast Hollandaise Sauce

Ingredients

4 oz/100 g butter
3 egg yolks
¼ teaspoon salt
few grains cayenne pepper
1 tablespoon lemon juice

Method

1 Beat the egg yolks with a wooden spoon until smooth but not fluffy.
2 Add seasoning and lemon juice.
3 In a separate pan melt the butter, then stir in the eggs.
4 Add 3 tablespoons hot water.
5 Place in a double boiler of hot (but not boiling) water.
6 Stir until thick (about 5 minutes).
7 Set aside until ready to use, then reheat over hot water. Serve lukewarm.

Family Favourite

Kedgeree

What memsahibs used to have for tiffin in the days of the Indian Empire. But you can eat it anytime.

Ingredients

6 oz/175 g cooked fresh haddock
6 oz/175 g cooked smoked haddock
6 oz/175 g long grain rice
3 oz/75 g butter
2 large hardboiled eggs, chopped
4 tablespoons fresh single cream
salt and pepper

Method

1 Boil, rinse and strain the rice. Spread over a big serving dish and leave in a low oven to dry.
2 Flake the cooked fish.
3 Melt the butter in a large saucepan, add fish, rice, eggs and cream.
4 Mix quickly. Add a little more cream if the mixture seems too dry.
5 Season to taste.
6 Place mixture in buttered ovenproof dish and cover with lid or foil.
7 Reheat on Mark 3/325°F/160°C for 20–30 minutes. The rice should be hot but not crusty.

JULY

Monday
25

Tuesday
26

Mick Jagger is 33 today (born 1944).
Another horsey week: Goodwood starts in West Sussex.
Good grounds for a picnic.

Wednesday
27

Thursday
28

Third Test Match at Trent Bridge.

Friday
29

Saturday
30

Cowes Week begins. Millionaires ahoy!

Sunday
31

Supertip
If you feel liverish, squeeze the juice of a lemon and knock it back on one gulp, first thing in the morning (ancient Greek cure).

Supertip
If you think you have a valuable antique picture, the National Gallery will tell you whether you have or not, though they won't value it or help you to sell it. Similarly, the Victoria and Albert Museum or the British Museum will advise you on the date and history of antique objects free of charge. Get a valuation from a top auctioneer such as Sothebys (34 New Bond Street, London W1). If you auction your item, put a reserve price on it at 10% more than your highest valuation. Valuations are always very pessimistic.

Traditional Dish

Very Delicious Redcurrant Jelly (Makes approximately 3 lb/1¼ kg)

Ingredients

6 lb/2½–3 kg redcurrants (or red and white mixed)

1¼ lb/550 g sugar per pint/6 dl juice (see step 4 below)

Raspberry Jelly

Make as above, substituting raspberries for redcurrants, but use 1 lb/450 g sugar to each pint/6 dl of juice. It will need slightly longer boiling than the redcurrant jelly before setting point is reached.

Method

1 Stem and wash the fruit. Pull them through the prongs of a fork to remove stalks. Heat slowly in a wide preserving pan until the currants are soft (about 45 minutes), stirring gently and frequently.

2 Simmer 2–3 minutes, then mash in pan or put through blender.

3 Pour into scalded jelly bag and leave overnight.

4 Measure the juice and add 1¼ lb/550 g preserving sugar to each pint/6 dl.

5 When sugar is dissolved, bring to boil stirring constantly and boil rapidly for a full minute.

6 Skim and pour into warm jars before it has time to set in the pan.

Reputation Maker

Edwardian Devilled Kidneys (Good to sail home to)

Ingredients

4 lamb's kidneys

1 teaspoon chopped onion (or more, depending on taste)

2–4 mushrooms

salt and pepper

¼ pint/1½ dl stock

1 teaspoon flour

2 tablespoons sherry

squeeze of lemon juice

a good pinch of English mustard

4 slices hot buttered toast or fried bread

Method

1 Skin and remove core from kidneys, wash, dry and slice.

2 Over a low heat melt butter and fry chopped onion. When golden brown, add sliced mushrooms and then kidneys, cook for about 5 minutes.

3 Add flour, mix well and gradually add stock, sherry, lemon juice, mustard and seasoning to taste.

4 Cook for several minutes and serve on buttered toast or fried bread.

August

ARIES

A curious situation now arises in your solar horoscope due to the fact that both the Sun and Saturn are currently in Leo, your angle of romantic attachments. The Sun is expansive, outgoing and happy-making while Saturn represents sacrifices, limitations and restrictions – find your own common denominator; in fact, it's an astrologer's nightmare trying to decide which influence is most effective. Place your bets on Saturn and be prepared for a month when you will be either in a temper or in tears. The time around the 13th and 15th will be the most decisive and only you can decide whether or not you have the desire and the stamina to battle on. If a break or separation does occur, ensure that all financial arrangements you are expected to accept are watertight and even partnerships remain intact.

TAURUS

Developments close to home and within the family circle will give you the greatest number of headaches and sleepless nights this August and it will need all that Taurian willpower and determination to keep your temper under control. The Sun close to Saturn in Leo is the protagonist but an adverse aspect to Uranus in your opposite sign of Scorpio is probably the most disruptive factor. Make up your mind that partners will be both pernickety and perverse and soldier on. It must be boring to be thought of only as the builder and organizer when you have in fact a considerable amount of artistic and creative talent. But isn't it your own fault that you are underestimated? When Jupiter enters Cancer on August 22 you are afforded an opportunity to prove just how inventive you can be.

GEMINI

Alexander Pope, a fellow-Geminian, wrote 'True wit is nature to advantage dressed, What oft was thought, but ne'er so well expressed.' However, you're going to find it unusually difficult to express your thoughts, ideas and feelings this month and relatives in particular will imagine they are getting the brush-off – and probably they are, for with Saturn currently in a highly significant area of your solar horoscope, you no longer wish to be thought of as some kind of court jester. Saturn, well aspected as it is in your case, strengthens convictions and the desire to find rational and practical solutions to very intimate problems. Don't, however, believe that you can re-shape and reorganize your life overnight, though with Mars currently in your birthsign you should be at your most vital.

CANCER

All you have to do is believe that it's all going to be lovely, that the time has come to move onwards and upwards and for your heart to come out of exile, and the world's your oyster now. How about that for a statement to give you confidence? – but it's true. Venus enters your own birthsign on August 3 followed by Jupiter on the 21st and perhaps for the first time in many years you'll realize that your biggest mistake was that you expected a dividend from an emotional investment. Cancer is associated with the home, the base from which we all operate. Perhaps you should also now come to understand that – to quote an old Yorkshire saying – 'when children are young, they tug at your apron-strings, and when they leave you, they tug at your heartstrings.'

LEO

What is generosity? The ability to give freely, liberally – never being stingy, but always nobleminded, magnanimous: and it must be difficult for you to accept the fact that in the past you've been too generous. Now with both the Sun your ruler and Saturn together in your birth-sign, you must begin to face the painful truth that it's time to be more self-protective and not allow others to impose on you. In the final analysis, who pays the bills? Life for Leos ought to be a banquet but have you ever thought that you have a lot in common with people born under your opposite sign of Aquarius? But whereas Aquarians are cool, dispassionate and concerned with the world *en masse* you need only one person as the object of your affection.

VIRGO

There is a Dorothy Parker poem entitled 'Ultimatum' and August is about this.

I'm wearied of wearying love, my friend,
Of worry and strain and doubt;
Before we begin let us view the end,
And maybe I'll do without.
There's never the pang that was worth the tear,
And toss in the night, I won't –
So either you do or you don't, my dear,
Either you do or you don't.
The table is ready, so lay your cards
And if they should augur pain,
I'll tender you ever my kind regards
And run for the fastest train.
I haven't the will to be spent and sad;
My heart's to be gay and true –
Then either you don't or you do, my lad,
Either you don't or you do!

LIBRA

Somewhere in the Koran you'll find these words – 'it is better to sit alone than in the company of fools'. Maybe by sitting alone this August you'll begin to realize how much you've depended on the company of fools and that the moment is right to accept this concept. There are only two kinds of people – those who kiss and those who turn their cheek to be kissed. What do you want? What do you expect? The current planetary situation compels you to answer both of these questions and answer them truthfully. If you want success, achievement and recognition, it is yours for the asking but somehow you have to re-evaluate and reassess relationships. The Sun, terribly close to Saturn, takes you back into the past and makes you retrace your tracks or go over ground you've already covered.

SCORPIO

If you care to spend a moment and read the predictions and prognostications for this month, you'll realize that there's an enormous kind of sea-change occurring which possibly can only be described by plagiarizing the words of poets and writers. But how does one tell a Scorpio anything? It's Scorpios who think they alone tell the truth, but the disappointments and disasters you've experienced in the past were due to the fact that you mistimed your truth sessions. No one has been quite ready for your brand of honesty! Don't worry about what is said or implied now. The most important thing is to face the ultimate truth, which is that you can't, under any circumstances, be restrained or held back. Jupiter in Cancer from August 21 makes it possible for you to find the courage.

SAGITTARIUS

At last, at last – the end of those matrimonial and partnership battles is in sight. Both Jupiter and Venus move out of your opposite sign of Gemini this month and it only remains for Mars to do the same at the beginning of September and you can settle down to a more tranquil and contented life. It's been a long haul and probably at times a very depressing one, but you should have learned a thing or two about the value of relationships and that in future you must be less critical if you want to keep them intact. Both the Sun and Saturn in Leo this month emphasize travel plans and arrangements. However, whenever Saturn is involved, limitations and restrictions seem to be the order of the day. Financial affairs and business interests are under beneficial aspects and it would be the right time to settle long outstanding legal disputes.

CAPRICORN

On August 3 Venus enters your opposite sign of Cancer, followed by Jupiter on the 21st – and both will be. at an adverse angle to Pluto in the area of your career and professional interests. This points to a break in a partnership or close involvement and may even lead to a change of occupation. Another important planetary factor this month relates to joint finances and business arrangements. The Sun close to your ruler Saturn signifies that you are bound to experience a considerable amount of difficulty in collecting what's due to you and will therefore be hard-pressed to fulfil your commitments. All in all, a demanding month, but Capricorns do not know the meaning of the word defeat, and survive you will.

AQUARIUS

The Sun in Leo until August 24 will make partners and lovers that much more detached and unco-operative, which is saying a lot because Saturn, also now in Leo, has probably made you wonder whether in fact some relationships are worth pursuing. The choice isn't really yours, as you'll realize only too well around the 13th and 15th of the month, and if anyone is told to go it may just be you. You will, however, be appreciated and even idolized at work this month. Both Venus and Jupiter in Cancer make fantastic aspects to your own planetary ruler Uranus in Scorpio, and if ever there was a time when you could convince those in positions of strength and authority that you're a near genius, this is it.

PISCES

It should all begin to happen for you this month, and, with both Venus and Jupiter in your angle of romance and good fortune, just about anything can! Pisceans are always considered to be soft, pliable and changeable; this last quality is beautifully illustrated by Elizabeth Barrett Browning, who was of course a Piscean, in the verse –

'Yes,' I answered you last night;
'No,' this morning, sir, I say.
Colours seen by candle-light
Will not look the same by day.

But getting back to that romance and good fortune bit – between now and the end of the year you should begin to enjoy relationships rather than be overpowered or bewildered by them, and if your job enables you to express your artistic and creative abilities you should receive some kind of promotion or recognition now. If it doesn't, change it.

AUGUST

Monday
1

Bank Holiday in Scotland and Republic of Ireland.
Start of the silly season in newspaper offices.
Royal National Eisteddfod of Wales at Wrexham.

Motherlore
Watch for idiots frying eggs on
Air Ministry roof and renewed
sightings of Loch Ness Monster.

Tuesday
2

Supertip
Plan for Bank Holiday weekend
at end of the month.

Wednesday
3

Motherlore
Everyone is good for someone.
The difficulty is to know who
(and when).

Thursday
4

Harrogate Festival of Arts & Sciences (to August 17).

Motherlore
It's unreasonable to expect an
unreasonable man to be
reasonable.

Friday
5

Saturday
6

Motherlore
Everything is good for
something. The difficulty is to
know what.

Sunday
7

Supertip
Don't whip egg whites in a small
bowl – they stiffen more quickly
in a larger one.

Traditional Dish

The Bishop's Homemade Lemonade

A blender recipe. Makes 9 pints/5 litres.

Ingredients
- 6 lemons
- 6 dessertspoons caster sugar
- 1 cup boiling water
- 8 pints/4½ litres cold water

Method
1. Grate lemon peel and put aside.
2. Slit lemons and pulp in blender.
3. Transfer pulp to a saucepan, add grated peel and hot water. Leave for 1 hour, then strain the lemon juice.
4. Dissolve sugar in a little hot water. Add to lemon juice.
5. Add cold water, chill and serve.

Gardening

August Gardener

Lift onions and shallots, dry in the sun (hopefully) and store. Sow cabbage in seedbed outside for next spring and early summer.

Family Favourite

Salade Niçoise (Can be served as a starter or as a summer supper dish)

Ingredients
- 3 quartered tomatoes
- ½ small onion, peeled and finely sliced
- ½ green pepper, sliced
- handful of radishes
- 2 chopped stalks celery
- 4 anchovy fillets
- 1 hardboiled egg, quartered
- 5 black olives
- 1 crushed clove of garlic
- tin of tuna fish
- 4 tablespoons French dressing with added pinch of basil

Method
1. Mix dressing, beating with a fork until the mixture thickens slightly.
2. Mix salad and dressing in a large bowl.

AUGUST

Monday
8

Tuesday
9

Wednesday
10

Thursday
11

Fourth Test Match at Headingley.

Friday
12

The glorious – grouse shooting starts.

Saturday
13

Sunday
14

Home rule
She who cooks does not wash up if there's anyone else in sight.

How to crunch ice
Wrap in a clean teatowel and bash gently with an empty milk bottle on a wooden board.

Motherlore
Everyone feels inadequate – not just you.

Supertip
If double cream tastes a bit 'off' make a sour cream dressing by adding the juice of half a lemon to 1 small carton of cream or yoghurt. Add salt and pepper and 1 clove of crushed garlic. Stir well. This makes a good dressing for shrimp or other seafood salads, especially if you add a couple of tablespoons of tomato ketchup.
Alternatively, sourish cream can be served with sweet fruit such as mulled strawberries, raspberries or apricots.

Motherlore
Haste makes waste and waste makes want.

Family Favourite

Cheese and Asparagus Tart
Ingredients
4 oz/100 g shortcrust pastry
4 oz/100 g grated cheese
1 tin asparagus spears
1 oz/25 g butter
1 oz/25 g flour
½ pint/3 dl milk
salt and pepper

Method
1 Line an 8-inch/21-cm flan ring with the pastry, trim edges and fill with a piece of crumpled foil or beans, to help flan keep shape during cooking.
2 Bake at the top of a hot oven Mark 7/425°F/220°C for 15–20 minutes until the pastry is cooked, but not brown in colour.
3 Melt the butter, stir in flour and cook for 2–3 minutes.
4 Remove pan from heat and gradually add liquid. Bring to boil and carry on stirring until sauce has thickened.
5 Remove from heat, stir in 3 oz/75 g of the cheese, and season.
6 Drain asparagus spears, place in pastry case, putting aside one or two for decoration; pour sauce over asparagus.
7 Sprinkle remaining cheese over and brown under a hot grill.
8 Garnish with remaining asparagus and serve.

Family Favourite

Pussyfoot
(An exotic frothy cocktail much ordered by model girls, who don't want their escorts to realize that their diets forbid alcohol)

Ingredients
2 oz/50 ml fresh lemon juice
2 oz/50 ml fresh orange juice
1 oz/25 ml lime juice
teaspoonful of whipped egg white

Method
Whip together. Garnish glass with orange or lemon slice.

AUGUST

Monday
15

Tuesday
16

Wednesday
17

Thursday
18

Robert Redford is 40 today (born 1937).

Friday
19

Saturday
20

Three Choirs Festival at Gloucester (to August 28).
They're celebrating the 250th anniversary.
It's the oldest surviving music festival in Europe.

Sunday
21

Edinburgh Festival starts (to September 10).
Football season starts, while they're still having cricket Test
Matches. Here we go again . . .

Motherlore
First day of Ramadan, the Islamic holy month of fasting. Rather like Christian Lent or Jewish Yom Kippur. Moslems must abstain from food, drink and sex all month during daylight hours. Dusk to dawn things proceed as usual. Fasting begins and ends when new moon is sighted. If skies are clouded and moon cannot be seen, all proceedings are delayed until moon is visible. Ramadan ends with festival of fast-breaking.

Supertip
Haven't chopped parsley for years. De-stalk parsley, put it in a clear little plastic bag and freeze in the ice compartment. Whenever you want to add that professional touch to some savoury dish just scrunch the frozen parsley bag above the dish and it chops as it scatters.

Motherlore
Everyone is difficult, especially men.

Motherlore
Life is untidy.

Supertip
To keep your table silver polished, mix 1 tablespoon of ammonia with 1 teaspoon of silver plate powder and 1 cup of water. Soak a cloth in this mixture and hang it up until quite dry. Then use it to dry your silver.

Family Favourite

Cutlets of Pork in Cider

Ingredients

4 pork cutlets
$\frac{1}{4}$ pint/$1\frac{1}{2}$ dl dry cider
$\frac{1}{8}$ pint/$\frac{3}{4}$ dl water
1 tablespoon flour
1 clove garlic, crushed
sprig of rosemary
salt and pepper
a few capers

Method

1 Brown cutlets on both sides in a little dripping or pork fat.
2 Remove, add flour to the fat in the pan and cook until golden.
3 Add the cider and water, and cook for 2–3 minutes.
4 Put cutlets into the sauce, add seasoning, garlic and rosemary (which can be removed later).
5 Cover pan and cook in slow oven Mark 3/325°F/160°C for 30 minutes.
6 Add a few capers to the sauce before serving with boiled potatoes, noodles or rice.

Reputation Maker

The Duchess of Windsor's Prawns Creole

Ingredients

1 medium onion, cut finely
1–2 cloves garlic, crushed
1 oz/25 g butter
2 dessertspoons tomato paste
1 tablespoon flour
1 tin peeled tomatoes
1 large green pepper
8 oz/225 g peeled prawns
2–3 teaspoons lemon juice
2 teaspoons Worcester sauce
salt and pepper

Method

1 Fry the onion and garlic gently in the butter until just turning colour.
2 Mix in the flour and stir until golden brown.
3 Add tomato paste, tomatoes, peppers and prawns. Bring to simmering point and season.
4 Cook slowly for 20 minutes, covering pan.
5 When cooked, add Worcester sauce and lemon juice to taste. Serve in a ring of fluffy rice. (Make the ring by piling it up with a serving spoon.)

AUGUST

Monday
22

Apply for prospectus for evening classes. Decide which.

Tuesday
23

Wednesday
24

Thursday
25

Children go back to school soon. Start checking clothes and books.
Fifth Test Match at the Oval.

Friday
26

Saturday
27

Sunday
28

Supertip
Fit your packet of washing powder into a plastic bag to protect it from wet hands.

To repair a zip temporarily
Pull it up and then slap a bit of Sellotape either across or up it (also good for a temporary hem).

To repair a zip broken at the base
Pull down the slide below the fractured teeth; cut them out. Then run slide above the gap, engaging the teeth on both sides. Stitch the zip together firmly just above the broken area.

Supertip
If there is a danger of plaster cracking when you're putting in a picture nail, first stick a piece of Sellotape over the plaster.

Morecambe Shrimp Soup

Ingredients

1 pint/6 dl cooked shrimps
½ lb/225 g white fish
1½ pints/scant litre fish stock
3 tablespoons white breadcrumbs
2 oz/50 g butter
1 onion
lemon peel/juice of half a lemon
herbs
salt and pepper
1 teacup cream (or milk)
1 egg yolk
pinch nutmeg

Method

1 Prepare stock by simmering the fish and shrimp shells, onion, herbs and lemon peel in 1½ pints/scant litre of water for about 20 minutes.
2 Strain, and add white breadcrumbs.
3 Pound shrimps in a mortar, with butter, adding lemon juice and nutmeg.
4 Gradually add the stock and the breadcrumbs until the mixture is creamy.
5 Heat mixture in a pan for 5 minutes, then put through a sieve or blender.
6 In a separate bowl beat the egg yolk and cream together and stir in 2 or 3 tablespoons of the hot soup.
7 Return mixture to the pan and stir until hot, but do not let it boil.

Classic Chocolate Mousse

Ingredients

8 oz/225 g plain chocolate
4 eggs
1 tablespoon rum or brandy or Tia Maria (optional)

Method

1 Separate the eggs and beat the yolks. Put aside.
2 Melt the chocolate in a pan over a low flame with a tablespoon water, or a tablespoon rum, etc.
3 Stir until smooth.
4 Stir melted chocolate into the egg yolks.
5 Whip egg whites until stiff and peaky and fold into the chocolate, so that the whole mixture is well blended.
6 Put mousse into a soufflé dish or individual ramekins and leave in a cool place to set.

September

ARIES

Last month it was the Sun close to Saturn in Leo which made you delve deep into your emotions in an attempt to find the complete and utter truth about yourself and your feelings. Now it's Venus which comes along to ensure that you have learnt something of lasting value. Work matters may be in a pickle and certainly while Mercury is in retrograde motion until the 15th you shouldn't pin your hopes on promises of promotion or recognition, but in the final analysis it'll be very personal and private issues which bewilder and frustrate you this September. The Sun enters your opposite sign of Libra on the 24th and as it moves closer to Pluto any form of partnership or alliance needs to be handled with the greatest amount of care, tact and patience. As an Arian you need a lot of change and variety.

TAURUS

Although the Sun has now moved into a favourable angle and you should be slowly beginning to get home and domestic difficulties in their right perspective, you can't afford to be nonchalant about family commitments and obligations because Saturn continues to exert its baleful influence and every time you step out of line you're made to realize there's just no escape. However, at least the Sun in Virgo until the 23rd makes you more self-reliant and optimistic. Mars has been bedevilling your financial fortunes since early July but after September 2 its effect is constructive rather than destructive. Maybe this is the right time to talk about Jupiter in Cancer; between now and the end of the year you'll be filled with an enormous desire to express your thoughts, ideas and feelings.

GEMINI

Each year while the Sun in Virgo is at an adverse angle to your birthsign you should plan a holiday or remove yourself from your usual environment because you are too emotionally vulnerable and easily hurt by the antics and antagonistic behaviour of those who are supposed to be your nearest and dearest. This year is no exception; in fact, because your own ruling planet Mercury is in retrograde motion until the 15th you are likely to over-react and over-dramatize situations. Saturn continues to exert an enormous influence on your thinking and outlook – seldom have you ever wanted so many 'i's' dotted and 't's' crossed. However, try to understand that relatives and associates also are entitled to explanations, and that if conflicts and disputes are to be avoided you must be prepared to take them into your confidence.

CANCER

Now you really can't complain. Not only has Jupiter entered your own birthsign but after September 2 Mars will also be in Cancer. Mars endows one with energy and the determination to surmount obstacles; true, it also makes one a little too impulsive and outrageous, but who cares? Isn't it about time you crept out of that crab-like shell and, like Noel Coward's Mrs Wentworth-Brewster, discovered in the nick of time that life is for living? You won't need, however, to journey as far as a bar on the Piccolo Marina to find romance, excitement and adventure. In fact, it will all be there for the taking. Of course every month is not without its dreary moments and with Venus and Saturn in your angle of finances you may be forced to scratch around to pay the milkman – oh, give him a cheque.

LEO

Percy Bysshe Shelley – one of your lot – wrote: 'Fate, Time, occasion, chance and change? To these all things are subject but eternal love.' Remember it this month when nothing seems to go right and when you begin to wonder why is there ever goodbye? Venus close to Saturn in your own birthsign means the party's over and certainly until Mars enters Leo at the end of October you are not going to feel anything like your radiant self. Reflect, ponder and reassess situations as much as you like – you will still come up with the same answer. It is not others who have changed but you. A year from now Jupiter will transit Leo; in the meantime, you are expected to separate the chaff from the grain – keep what is worth keeping and, with a breath of kindness, blow the rest away.

VIRGO

Did you take Dorothy Parker's advice last month? Did you make it absolutely clear that enough is enough and that nothing can prevent you from doing your own thing now – no matter what it is? Whether you did or not, don't indulge yourself in emotional dramas this September even though you know you can get star billing. The Sun in Virgo until the 23rd makes you more forthright and volatile but unfortunately your own ruling planet Mercury is in retrograde motion until the 15th and therefore you are likely to be misinformed and easily misled. Virgo people are invariably presented as prim, painstaking and slightly petty but few really know you because you are so utterly private and personal and not given to making a great display of your emotions.

LIBRA

Now it really is work time. Mars and Jupiter together at the zenith of your solar horoscope bid you set your sights that much higher and devote more attention to your career. Anyway, friendships and close relationships could be too complicated and demanding for you to really enjoy yourself so you might just as well concentrate on another kind of security. Don't, however, be in too much of a rush to make important professional changes. Mercury in retrograde motion until September 15 indicates that you should do a lot of homework first – facts presented are likely to be misleading and not the complete truth by a long chalk. Librans are fundamentally heart people but you are easily turned off. Around mid-month when your own ruler Venus is close to Saturn you will begin to realize just how impractical and unrealistic you have been about affairs of the heart.

SCORPIO

September looks as if it's going to be a busy, and in some respects, decisive month for you: busy, because both Mars and Jupiter will be in the area of your solar horoscope which relates to long-distance travel and involvement with people from other lands; decisive, because Venus and Saturn accentuate career and professional matters to an almost alarming degree. You have probably been aware for a long time that to make any real headway now you must make some kind of complete break with the past and it will most likely be around mid-month that an opportunity occurs for you to do just that. Both personal and partnership finances should begin to improve.

SAGITTARIUS

With both the Sun and Mercury making difficult aspects to your natal Sun in Sagittarius this September, it would be wise and politic for you to stay out of the limelight for a while and re-evaluate situations. However, the overall picture is certainly an encouraging one, but, because you were born under a Fire sign, having made your mind up that you want something, you want it instantly. Better by far to take a deep breath, curb your impatience and consider only long-term prospects. The difficult phase in matrimonial and partnership conflicts is definitely over now, but you must realize that others cannot as yet forget what has transpired or give you their complete trust – they will eventually. Your own ruler Jupiter in Cancer is now joined by Mars and financial arrangements with others are more straightforward and you seem to have the advantage.

CAPRICORN

It does seem a little unfair that no matter how hard you try to do the right thing, all your attempts to please and placate partners are to no avail. Now, because Mars enters your opposite sign of Cancer on September 2, it would be foolish to presume that you will fare any better this month or find permanent solutions to emotional problems. However, with the Sun and Mercury in Virgo there will be at least some light relief although you'll have to travel far away from your usual environment to find any real peace of mind. A typical Capricorn knows the art of timing, how to grasp opportunities and make the most of situations, but the boat really does get rocked when emotional disturbances occur.

AQUARIUS

Emotionally and financially a complex month, due to the fact that Venus will be together with Saturn in your opposite sign of Leo, and until the 15th Mercury in retrograde motion will confuse all partnership or joint financial arrangements. But it is the Venus/Saturn combination which has to be watched. If you consider the nature of these two planets – Venus, jolly, romantic and even flirtatious, overpowered by the dour, demanding and rather depressing Saturn – you will understand that now more than ever you are expected to conform. Fulfil your obligations and don't for a second tip the scales, no matter how aggrieved and hard-done-by you feel. Fortunately important and beneficial career changes are on the horizon and here at least your opinions and ideas will be respected.

PISCES

In spite of the unusual number of adverse aspects relating to matrimonial and partnership affairs, September should be quite an exhilarating and rewarding month. Jupiter, Mars and Uranus occupy strong enough positions in your solar horoscope to enable you to see beyond current domestic difficulties and give you the confidence to inform others that your talents and abilities can no longer remain suppressed. It is, however, a month when you must face up to some harsh realities, and if your attributes are to be recognized you must deliver the goods. Longfellow of course was the perfect Piscean. He realized, that 'in this world a man must be either anvil or hammer'. But most pertinent of all this month is his dictate – 'If you would hit the mark, you must aim a little above it.'

Monday
29

Bank Holiday in England, Northern Ireland and Wales.
Last holiday this summer. Enjoy it. September is a busy month.

Tuesday
30

Wednesday
31

Thursday
1

Conker season about to start.
Partridge shooting begins.
Oyster season opens.

Friday
2

VJ Day. World War II ended in 1945 with victory over Japan.
School holidays nearly over.

Saturday
3

Royal Highland Gathering at Braemar.
First blackberries should be ripening.

Sunday
4

Harvest Festival.

Motherlore
Why not put yourself on a
mental diet of non-interference?

Make your own convenience food
Shortcrust pastry mixture, before
the water has been added, can be
stored for up to five days in a jar
in the fridge; this makes for a
lighter pastry. It can also be
stored in this way with added
sugar and used as a crumble top.

Reputation Maker

Rosie's Lemon Sorbet
Ingredients
$\frac{1}{2}$ pint/3 dl lemon juice
$\frac{1}{2}$ lb/225 g sugar
$\frac{3}{4}$ pint/4 dl water

Method
1 Make a syrup by boiling the water and sugar quickly together for 5 minutes.
2 Cut the tops off the lemons carefully and scoop out flesh. Do not break the skins – best to do it with a teaspoon or grapefruit knife. (If you don't want to serve the sorbet in lemon cups, simply squeeze lemons in usual way and freeze sorbet in a plastic container.)
3 Get as much juice as possible from the pulp by pushing through a nylon sieve.
4 Add the juice to the cooled syrup and freeze for 1–2 hours, by which time the mixture should be fairly mushy.
5 Turn into a blender or bowl and beat well.
6 Spoon the mixture into the lemon shells, letting it come slightly over the top.
7 Press the lids on, wipe the outside to remove stickiness, and freeze again in an upright position for about 1 hour.
8 Remove from freezer 10–15 minutes before serving.

Gardening

September Gardener
Lift potatoes when haulm (that's what the green part is called when it withers) is decayed. Allow to dry off for a few hours and store in the dark (or they go green and become poisonous).

Garden Bulbs
Plant outdoor crocuses in September (3–4 inches deep, 2 inches apart).
Plant outdoor daffodils in September/October (3–4 inches deep, 6 inches apart).
Plant outdoor irises in September/October (3–4 inches deep, 6 inches apart).
Plant outdoor snowdrops in September/October (3–4 inches deep, 6 inches apart).
Plant outdoor hyacinths in September/November (4–6 inches deep, 9 inches apart).

SEPTEMBER

Monday
5

Check enrolment days for evening classes at your local library.

Tuesday
6

Wednesday
7

Thursday
8

Friday
9

Saturday
10

St Leger at Doncaster.

Sunday
11

Spiced Vinegar

Now's the time to prepare your spiced vinegar ready for autumn pickling. You need 1 quart/ generous litre of white or malt vinegar and ½ oz/7 g of each of the following spices: whole cinnamon, cloves, allspice, whole bruised ginger and white peppercorns. Just put the spices in the vinegar to steep and leave for 1–2 months in a corked or screw-top bottle. Shake the bottle from time to time – whenever you remember. Strain the vinegar before using. (Increase or decrease ingredients proportionately according to how much you're going to need.)

If you want spiced vinegar quickly, there's a near-instant method: put the spices and vinegar into a bowl, cover and stand in a saucepan of cold water. Bring the water to the boil, then take the pan off the heat and leave the vinegar and spices for about 2 hours. Strain before use.

To make spiced vinegar syrup – for pickling peaches for instance (see page 189) – leave out the peppercorns and add 2 lb/900 g sugar to each pint/6 dl of spiced vinegar when you need to use it.

Family Favourite

Ratatouille A classic Mediterranean dish. Serve hot or cold.

Ingredients
1 onion, peeled and sliced

2 tomatoes, peeled and sliced

3 pimentos, thinly sliced, with stalks and seeds removed

2 aubergines, peeled and sliced in thin rounds

2 courgettes, peeled and sliced in thin rounds

4 tablespoons olive oil (although any cooking oil will do)

2 cloves garlic, peeled and crushed

thyme (preferably 2 fresh sprigs, otherwise 2 pinches)

salt and pepper

Method
1 Season vegetables. Heat olive oil in a saucepan and add all ingredients.
2 Simmer slowly until quite soft.
3 Add more oil if it sticks. Drain off any surplus oil if too runny.

Reputation Maker

Pickled Peaches

Ingredients
4 lb/1¾ kg peaches

1 pint/6 dl spiced vinegar syrup

preserving jars

September is the month to plan a mouthwatering winter store cupboard. *Pickle* walnuts. Grate and pickle horse-radish for making into relish or cream *Preserve* stone fruit.

Jam, *bottle* or *spice* plums, peaches, apricots, etc. Consider making damson cheese. Decide not to bother.

Make *jellies* from mulberries, wild blackberries, elder, japonica and rowan Also gather rose hips for *syrup*.

To make *chutneys and jams* gather wind-fall apples, pears, greengages and plums.

Method
1 Peel and quarter peaches, remove stones.
2 Poach in hot spiced vinegar syrup for 10 minutes or until tender.
3 Tightly pack the fruit into warm clean jars.
4 Boil syrup rapidly for 2–3 minutes to reduce it, remove scum and pour over fruit.
5 Seal immediately.

SEPTEMBER

Monday
12

Jewish New Year (Rosh Hashanah). It's the start of year 5738.
Liberal Assembly by the sea. It lasts until Saturday.
Chelsea Antiques Fair (to September 24).

Tuesday
13

Wednesday
14

Thursday
15

Friday
16

Saturday
17

Sunday
18

Motherlore
Why not be more selfish?

Motherlore
It's getting more and more
important to differentiate
between problems and
irritations. Only worry about
problems.

Supertip
Plan your power cut now. Buy
torch, candles and little spirit
stove. Winterize the car. Get
anti-freeze, check battery and
oil. Get rust treatment if you can
afford it.

Reputation Maker

Pears Baked in Cream

Ingredients

4 ripe pears
lemon juice
butter
$\frac{1}{2}$ pint/3 dl double cream
4 tablespoons sugar
2–3 drops vanilla essence
salt

Method

1 Peel, halve and core the pears.
2 Brush with lemon juice and put them, cut side down, in a buttered baking dish.
3 Combine the cream with half the sugar, vanilla essence and pinch of salt. Pour over the pears.
4 Sprinkle with remaining sugar.
5 Bake in a slow oven Mark 2/300°F/150°C for 30 minutes or until pears are tender. Serve hot.

Family Favourite

Devilled Chicken (Best made the day before) Serve hot or cold.

Ingredients

1 boiling fowl
2 small onions
2 small carrots
bouquet garni
peppercorns
salt

Sauce

1 tablespoon onion, finely chopped
2 tablespoons Worcester sauce
1 tablespoon tarragon vinegar
2–3 thin slices lemon, halved
1 clove garlic
1 cup tinned or fresh tomatoes, skinned and chopped
salt and pepper
1 bayleaf
1 cup chicken stock

Method

1 Simmer boiling fowl until tender with vegetables, bouquet garni and seasoning.
2 Leave fowl in the liquor until cold, then skin and joint into pieces.
3 Brush chicken pieces with melted butter, and grill quickly on both sides until brown.
4 Lay in a casserole.
5 Make the sauce by simmering all the sauce ingredients together for 10 minutes.
6 Pour the sauce over the chicken joints and leave until the next day so that the flavour of the sauce is fully absorbed. Serve with fluffy rice.

SEPTEMBER

Monday
19

Pete Murray's birthday. He's 52 (born 1925).

Tuesday
20

Wednesday
21

Thursday
22

Yom Kippur. Jewish Day of Atonement.
A day of fasting and prayers for forgiveness of past
transgressions plus resolutions to do better in future.

Friday
23

Autumn begins officially. It's the autumnal equinox, when the
sun enters the sign Libra and crosses from north to south of the
equator, making day and night equal all over the world.

Saturday
24

Sunday
25

Supertip
Salt runner (stick) beans for
winter.
Buy dried fruit for Christmas
cooking.
You're supposed to make your
mincemeat now. But nobody
will know if you buy it from a
shop and add extra brandy.

Motherlore
Self-sacrifice is often self-
indulgence.

Supertip
To coat meat, fish, etc. with
flour, place all ingredients in a
bag or plastic box with a fitting
lid and shake gently until each
piece is well coated.

Household Hint

Check your SNUG FOR WINTER list

Check electric blankets (do you need a time switch?). Consider getting electrician in to check all electrical appliances whether or not they're giving trouble. Fix weatherstrip around door and window gaps. Buy Chamberlain's Metal Weatherstrip, Durastrip or Semaster Do-it-Yourself Weather and Draught Proofing. Don't waste your money on plastic foam strips, unless you only want them to last one winter. To keep rain and draughts from the outside doors buy a device called the Sealmaster.

External check for: cracked chimney stacks/broken or missing roof tiles/brickwork needing repointing/ill-fitting skylight/leaks at gutter points. Free gutter outlet of birds' nests and – later – autumn leaves.

Consider insulating loft (one-third heat is lost this way). If any sash cords go this winter replace hemp with nylon.

Gardening

How to Grow Indoor Bulbs

(Crocuses, Daffodils, Tulips, Snowdrops, Hyacinths)

Plant in September/October, the larger the better, and buy special bulb fibre at the same time, because it will remain fresh throughout the growing season.

If you want Christmas flowering buy bulbs marked 'pre-cooled' or 'prepared'. Plant immediately after purchasing. Place layer of fibre at bottom of pot (don't press down) then press bulb in the fibre, then add more fibre so that bulb tips just show above final fibre level. Put in a cool dark place at a temperature of about 55°F/13°C (but not in airing cupboard, it's much too warm). Keep fibre moist until young shoots show 2–3 inches (takes about 8–12 weeks), then bring into normal temperature in shade. Keep damp.

Superwoman Competition

'Well, I wouldn't be here if I didn't, would I?'

What did the man mean?

Send the answer to me, on a postcard, together with your favourite home hint on how to save time, money and trouble.

PRIZES will be free copies of *Superwoman*, the bestseller book of home management. Write to Shirley Conran, c/o Sidgwick & Jackson, 1 Tavistock Chambers, Bloomsbury Way, London WC1A 2SG.

October

ARIES

You may not feel like persevering to find permanent solutions to matrimonial and partnership problems, but persevere you must. The Sun, Venus and Mercury will all at times be close to Pluto in your opposite sign of Libra and it is Pluto which makes you persistently aware that you'll have no real peace of mind until you either make relationships perfect or end them. In fact, the entire planetary set-up this month seems to focus on involvements and the need to know for certain where your emotions and devotions lie. Let it be said that Arians do try, and try hard, to support and encourage others, but you are by nature instant people and just as Mars your ruler needs to be tempered by Venus, you in turn should take a leaf out of the Libran book and not get so het up when folk do not act as you would wish.

TAURUS

If you are the Builder of the Zodiac, you need to put in a lot of overtime this month. The accent is on dreary, mundane things – career prospects and security. This, at a time when you are very much under par physically or having to cope with family health problems. It is in a way a marking time period when it is better to plod along rather than to believe that you can, with perseverance, make others accept your point of view. Two planets – Saturn and Uranus – are at adverse positions to your natal Sun in Taurus and therefore you are in a bit of a cleft stick. Saturn signifies responsibilities from which there is no escape while Uranus in Scorpio makes partners unaware of your emotional needs. It will be after the Sun also enters Scorpio on the 24th that they display their true colours.

GEMINI

October should be a fun month, and whatever else happens your heart will be taking a joy-ride. The Sun, Venus and your own planetary ruler Mercury in Libra accentuate emotions and, for want of a better phrase, you love life. However, other adverse planetary aspects indicate that financial obligations and commitments may prevent you from becoming too dangerously involved, which means to say, enjoy yourself but watch it! Relations and close associates can't wait to criticize and haul you over the coals, but if you think you are entitled to a measure of merry-making then don't allow anyone to discourage or disillusion you. Work? – well, the omens are good. The relationship between Jupiter and Uranus implies that all the changes now taking place are ones for the better.

CANCER

With Mars in your own birthsign until October 26 you are going to feel the time has come to stop pretending and call a spade a spade. Why not let the family and relations know that you are entitled to a certain amount of privacy and the freedom to live life as you choose? It really is going to be an eye-opener if you become what you want to be rather than the person others imagine you to be. All of the major planetary movements now occur in the lower half of your solar horoscope, meaning you don't give a damn about prestige, success or acclaim any longer; all you want is peace and the opportunity to do your own thing. Jupiter currently in Cancer builds and sustains you. Seldom have you been in such a strong position to tell others to push off.

LEO

It was Voltaire who said 'there is but one morality as there is but one geometry.' Now you must decide what is moral – not just in your financial dealings with others but also in relation to your emotions. It really is 'sort-out time'. You either put up or shut up; not an experience the true Leo will relish – you always prefer to give others the benefit of the doubt. You want people to live up to the identikit you have made of them, but sadly, it just does not fit any longer. Saturn now in Leo is teaching you to tell what are laughingly called 'home truths'; not just to lovers, friends and associates, but to yourself. If, as is likely to be the case, you feel let down, used and misunderstood, then have the courage to say so ere October is out. Maybe those who care most about you will, in the nick of time, appreciate your honesty.

VIRGO

A cursory glance at the past months' predictions will enlighten you on one score at least. So far, it has been a treacherous year for finances. Now you must face the bald truth – you really can't afford to procrastinate and play around any longer. Friendships and relationships have to be rebuilt on firmer and finer ground. Anyway, why should you always pick up the tab, check, bill – call it what you will? Mercury, your ruler, will be in Libra – your angle of income and personal finances – between October 5 and 21 and this is the time to settle a lot of accounts and old scores. You are going through an incredible phase of enlightenment: seldom has everything seemed so clear and well-defined. Enjoy it: believe in it.

LIBRA

Goethe – who was in fact born under Virgo – wrote, 'He who asks too much and enjoys complexities is likely to fall into error', a quote you should pin over your bed this October in the hope that when you are tempted to complicate situations and over-indulge yourself you will realize that it is you and you alone who are screwing things up. Jupiter at the midheaven point of your solar horoscope means the opportunities are there, but the Sun, Pluto and Mercury in Libra suggest you could become over-confident and complacent. Librans, as a race, are not good with money. But then, with Venus as your planetary ruler, you tend to believe you are protected – and so you are. But wouldn't it be nice for once to know that you can and should live a life without anticipating those final demands?

SCORPIO

It's not a question of hiding your light under a bushel this month, but you would be well advised to stay out of the limelight. The Sun, Pluto and Mercury all accentuate very private and personal matters, and what Scorpio would want them to become common knowledge? Maybe you should take a trip or holiday, a respite from everyday battles; certainly the planetary aspects indicate that you would be better off and more contented away from your accustomed environment. But the heartaches and soul-searching will go. Saturn in Leo gives you a greater longing for stability and security, but you must first find out where you went wrong The Sun enters your own birthsign on October 24, by which time you should be well on the way to sorting yourself and others out.

SAGITTARIUS

No matter who said 'The time has come!' you will know for sure there is no time like the present this month. But – and it is a big but – before you can move on to better things, you must concede that there are certain past debts and obligations which can no longer be ignored. Take a deep breath, fortify yourself with a large drink and admit you have made some mistakes. Then, and only then, will you find the support and security you need. Sagittarius is considered to be a lucky sign and you are certainly fortunate now in that even those you have antagonized or alienated in the past will be prepared to let bygones be bygones. October is a month in which to prove, undeniably and irrevocably, that you have not just talent, ability or even common sense – but generosity.

CAPRICORN

You are entitled to a lot of sympathy and consideration this month; if only you wouldn't carry on about difficulties, problems and disappointments you might get it. But the typical Capricorn has to tell the world just how unpleasant and unfair life is at the moment. This is a rather strong and sweeping statement, yet nevertheless valid. You do think it is your prerogative to tell the truth but if only you would realize how much you are valued, appreciated and loved, you could channel your energies in a more useful and fulfilling direction. October is one month when you can prove just how optimistic and uncomplaining you can be. Emotionally and professionally, you may have a lot of worries, but they are not to be exaggerated. Capricorn is symbolized by the mountain goat who does ultimately reach the summit.

AQUARIUS

Throughout 1977, no other sign – except perhaps Leo – has been lambasted by the planets more than Aquarius. Saturn and even your own ruler Uranus have continuously and mercilessly put you to the test. Now you begin to realize you are about to emerge, finer, stronger and more tolerant of others' deficiencies and idiosyncracies. It will, however, take a lot of courage on your part to pacify partners – partners meaning the people with whom you are involved emotionally, and from whom there is no escape. However, career matters should be going so well now that you can afford to make a lot of concessions and begin to believe that if you want someone to stay with you and share your experiences you have to tell them that they are needed. Try it; offer the olive branch and you won't need to build an Ark.

PISCES

Thank your lucky stars that you can swim in opposite directions this month – because it's the only way you will escape being hoist by your own petard and having to explain what you did with the money. The Sun and a lot of planetary activity in Libra indicate that if you have over-committed yourself you will now have to pay for your error of judgement. No point in pleading you were simply casting your bread upon the waters – it won't wash. However, it should be an exciting and exhilarating month emotionally. Mars and Jupiter together in Cancer mean it's party time and for once it's your turn to call the tune. Remember, however, that you have a job and career to think about, and if you are a wise Piscean you ensure that you get the recognition you deserve.

SEPTEMBER ~ OCTOBER

Monday
26

Tuesday
27

Wednesday
28

Brigitte Bardot is 43 today (born 1934).

Thursday
29

Michaelmas Day (Quarter Day—very confusing).

Friday
30

Saturday
1

Pheasant shooting starts.
Christmas is coming. You ought to start planning now.

Sunday
2

Supertip
Today, 3 years ago, Denis Healey (who was your Chancellor of the Exchequer at the time) said 'Inflation is currently 8·4%.' In fact it was 18% that year, or over twice as much. Old Mother Conran say listen *very* carefully to what the Chancellor says today.

Motherlore
Can't means won't and couldn't means wouldn't.

Supertip
Needing approval is an insatiable yearning. Ignore it.

Winter Warmer

Cream of Spinach Soup

Ingredients
- 1 lb/450 g washed fresh spinach (or ½ lb/ 225 g frozen)
- 1 or 2 small onions, peeled and chopped
- 1 small clove garlic, crushed
- 2 oz/50 g butter or margarine
- 1½ pints/scant litre of well-flavoured vegetable stock
- 3 tablespoons skimmed milk powder
- ½ pint/3 dl milk
- salt and pepper
- pinch of nutmeg

Method
1 Fry onions and garlic in butter for 5 minutes, being careful not to let them brown.
2 Add stock and spinach and cook steadily for about 25 minutes (if using frozen spinach only about 5 minutes).
3 Place in *warmed* liquidizer or run through mill.
4 Add salt, pepper and nutmeg, skimmed milk powder and milk, and blend until creamy.
5 Return to pan, correct seasoning and heat up ready for serving. Do not let mixture boil. Serve with croûtons.

Family Favourite

Ancient British Bubble and Squeak

(Bubble and squeak is generally considered to be leftover mashed potato and cabbage, heavily peppered and fried in hot dripping until brown. And very good it is too, but here is Dr Kitchiner's original recipe of 1823)

Ingredients
- a few slices of rather underdone cold boiled salted beef
- 2 oz/50 g butter
- 1 cabbage, boiled for 10 minutes and drained
- salt and pepper

Method
1 Heat butter in frying pan.
2 Pepper the slices of meat and fry lightly in heated butter.
3 Remove beef from frying pan, keep it hot on a plate over a saucepan of hot water.
4 Cut cabbage into small strips, pepper and salt, then toss it for 2–3 minutes in the frying pan. Pile up in the middle of a dish and surround it with the beef.

OCTOBER

Monday
3

Labour Party in conference at Brighton.
Horse of the Year Show at Wembley (to October 8).

Tuesday
4

Wednesday
5

Thursday
6

Friday
7

Saturday
8

Sunday
9

Supertip
On the whole, if you want to
know how a person will respond
to a suggestion, work out his
emotional response, not the
logical one. Emotion beats logic
90% of the time.

Family Favourite

Esau's Pottage

Ingredients

1 lb/450 g lentils (don't bother to soak them overnight)

2 quarts/2¼ litres salted water

½ lb/225 g peeled and sliced onions

2 lb/900 g tomatoes, peeled and chopped

dash of thyme and parsley

3 oz/75 g butter

1 oz/25 g grated cheese

Method

1 Boil lentils according to packet directions (which can be from ½–2 hours) until they are soft but not mushy.

2 Add onions, tomatoes and herbs.

3 Boil for further 10 minutes. Do not strain.

4 Add butter and cheese to melt before serving hot straightaway. It's not a soup that keeps.

Note: If I'm in a hurry I'm afraid I don't peel the tomatoes. Alternatively, I use tinned tomatoes and add the grated peel and juice of half a small orange.

Gardening

October Gardener

Do not remove dead heads of hydrangeas; they form valuable protection for next year's buds.

Lift and store root crops, except parsnips, which you dig up as you need them. Plant out good specimens of August-sown cabbage.

Family Favourite

Apple and Ginger Chutney

Ingredients

4 lb/1¾ kg cooking apples

1½ lb/675 kg soft brown sugar

4 oz/100 g crystallized ginger

or 2 level teaspoons ground ginger

2–3 cloves garlic, crushed

1 pint/6 dl vinegar

½ teaspoon mixed spice

cayenne pepper

1 teaspoon salt

Method

1 Peel, core and chop the apples. Boil for a few minutes with ½ pint/3 dl vinegar and the garlic until soft but not mushy.

2 Add remaining vinegar, ginger, sugar, mixed spice, pinch of cayenne and salt.

3 Continue cooking for a further 20 minutes or until thick.

4 Pour into warm clean jars and cover.

5 Leave for 2–3 months before using.

OCTOBER

Monday
10

Motherlore
Only the boring are bored.

Tuesday
11

Conservatives rally in Blackpool for their Annual Conference, until October 14.

Motherlore
'I suppose it's not the place's
  fault,' I said.
'Nothing, like something,
  happens anywhere . . .'
                    Philip Larkin

Wednesday
12

Thursday
13

Friday
14

Battle of Hastings lost 911 years ago today.

Overheard
1st small boy to 2nd small boy at party: 'Do you believe in the pill or French lettuces?'

Saturday
15

Sunday
16

Supertip
Don't worry about making an *unlumpy* sauce. Just make it, then beat it smooth in the saucepan with a hand whisk.

Traditional Dish

Cornish Pasties

Ingredients

8 oz/225 g shortcrust pastry
8 oz/225 g lean steak, finely chopped
4 oz/100 g raw potatoes, peeled and diced
1 small onion, finely chopped
salt and pepper
milk or eggs to glaze

Method

1 Roll out the pastry and divide into four rounds.
2 Mix steak, onion and potato and season. (My father, who was Cornish, always insisted on a very peppery taste.)
3 Divide mixture on to the four pastry rounds.
4 Damp the pastry edges and seal together.
5 Brush with milk or egg and prick the tops.
6 Bake at Mark 6/400°F/200°C for 30–40 minutes.

Family Favourite

Chicken Liver Pâté

Ingredients

½ lb/225 g chicken livers (frozen or fresh)
1 small shallot, finely chopped
1 oz/25 g butter
1 small clove garlic, peeled and crushed
2 sage leaves, or ½ teaspoon thyme leaves, finely chopped
dash of port, brandy, sherry or a little white wine
salt and pepper

This improves with keeping, but pour melted butter on top if it is to be kept for several days.

Method

1 Wash and trim chicken livers, chop into small pieces and sprinkle with salt and pepper.
2 Fry the shallot in the butter but do not let it brown.
3 Add chicken livers, herbs and garlic and turn the heat up a little, stirring constantly.
4 The livers should crumble as they cook. Keep mashing as you add the alcohol.
5 When livers are pinky-brown remove from heat and mash until smooth.
6 Put into a small dish or individual ramekins.
7 Serve, well chilled, with toast.

OCTOBER

Monday

State Opening of Parliament by the Queen will soon start new session.
MPs should be going back.

Tuesday

St Luke's Day. If it's warm, this time is known as St Luke's Summer.

Wednesday

Thursday
20

Friday
21

Trafalgar Day, 1805. We beat the French. Nelson's final victory.

Saturday

Tomorrow it will be 7 o'clock when it's 8 o'clock.
Early bedtime.

Sunday

British Summer Time ends. Clocks go back 1 hour after midnight today. So it'll be getting lighter earlier.

Supertip
Clean tiaras for State Openings and other real jewellery with a soft toothbrush in soapy water and dry quickly with tissue. Some clean their jewellery in gin but I'd rather drink it.

Supertip
To prevent carpets and rugs from curling up at the corners, stick a triangle of linoleum under each corner. Use Copydex, which is a fabric adhesive and won't make a nasty glue mark on the carpet.

Motherlore
If the doorbell or telephone rings . . . consider the food first. Either switch off the hobs or lift the food off. If you return fast it doesn't matter, but if you're faced with a sudden emergency you won't suddenly smell another one in the kitchen.

Traditional Dish

Irish Stew
Ingredients
2 lb/900 g middle neck or scrag of
  mutton
4 lb/1¾ kg potatoes, cut in half
1 lb/450 g onions, thickly sliced
bunch mixed herbs or teaspoon dried
  herbs
2 bayleaves
1 pint/6 dl water
salt and pepper

Method
1 Cut meat into cutlets and trim off fat.
2 In a large saucepan, put a layer of
  potatoes and onion, then a layer of
  meat, then more onion and potatoes,
  then meat again, etc. adding salt and
  pepper after each layer. Finally add all
  other ingredients.
3 Simmer gently for 2–2½ hours until
  meat is tender, shaking the pan from
  time to time to prevent sticking.

Reputation Maker

Pavlova Cake
Ingredients
3 egg whites
6 oz/175 g caster sugar
1 teaspoon cornflour
pinch of salt
1 teaspoon vinegar
½ teaspoon vanilla essence
about 1½ lb/675 g fresh soft fruit (washed,
  peeled, stoned and seeded) or bottled
  fruit: try grapes, peaches, plums,
  blackberries
whipped cream to garnish

Method
1 Line an 8-inch (21-cm) sandwich tin
  with greased paper.
2 Beat egg whites with salt until stiff and
  peaky.
3 Beat in half the sugar.
4 In a separate bowl mix cornflour with
  remaining sugar, then fold gently into
  egg whites.
5 Add vanilla essence and vinegar, then
  mix.
6 Spread into the prepared tin and bake
  slowly until firm on the outside but
  still soft inside (Mark 2/300°F/150°C,
  1 hour).
7 Turn upside down on a large serving
  dish and leave to cool.
8 Arrange the fruit on top and serve
  with cream.

OCTOBER

Monday
24

Time to plan your Christmas countdown. But of course you won't.

Supertip
Keep fuse wire and a torch on the fuse box itself, which is exactly where you're likely to need them. Pessimists would also keep a box of matches in case the torch battery is dead.

Tuesday
25

Battle of Agincourt. England's Henry V beat the French on their own ground.

Wednesday
26

Face flannels which become slimy due to an accumulation of soap can be boiled in a weak solution of vinegar (1 teaspoon per pint of water) for 10 minutes. Rinse in water to which you have added a few drops of ammonia, and then give a final rinse in clear water. As a preventative, launder flannels (in washing machine) weekly.

Thursday
27

Friday
28

Supertip
Remove stains from decanters and narrow-necked vases by soaking overnight in warm water with a tablespoon of biological detergent dissolved in it.

Saturday
29

Build up bonfire for Guy Fawkes night.
Get pumpkins for Hallowe'en, and candles, preferably with holders

Sunday
30

Hollow out pumpkins for Hallowe'en jack-o'-lanterns.
Make pumpkin soup.

Winter Warmer

Pumpkin Soup

Ingredients

1 3 lb/1½ kg pumpkin
2 oz/50 g butter
3 level tablespoons flour
2 small onions, peeled and sliced
1 pint/6 dl white stock
1 pint/6 dl milk
salt and pepper
2–3 tablespoons cream
2 oz/50 g grated cheese
chopped parsley for garnish

Method

1 Cut the pumpkin into bite-sized pieces, remove any seeds and soft core, remove peel.
2 Fry the onions and pumpkin in butter for about 5 minutes, until soft but not browned.
3 Put through a blender or sieve and return this soup to pan. Slowly stir in the white stock.
4 In a separate pan, blend the flour with a little of the milk to make a cream.
5 Add the remaining milk to the soup and reheat.
6 Stir a tablespoon of the soup into the creamed flour and milk, return mixture to pan.
7 Bring to the boil, stirring all the time until it thickens, and cook for 3 minutes.
8 Season to taste, add the cheese and cream, and sprinkle with parsley before serving.

Household Hint

Pickle onions and red cabbage.
Gather green tomatoes for chutney.
Pick quinces and store to ripen or make jelly.
Spice pears for Christmas.
Make goodies for spate of Charity Bazaars coming next month (e.g. fruit cakes to mature, sponge cakes to freeze, candies, pâtés, etc.). Also remember charity begins at home and stock your store cupboard.

Pick medlars and store to ripen for jelly.
Make Gingerbread Men, decorative candies, etc. for Christmas tree; store in airtight containers. Make Petit Fours for presents.
Plan any Christmas party. Date/guest list/invitations/food/drink/music/lighting/heating/where to put the coats/help.

November

ARIES

There is a lot of planetary activity in Leo and Scorpio this month and you may have to face up to some nasty emotional and financial problems. Your own ruler Mars together with Saturn in Leo makes you wonder whether or not your trust has been misplaced, while the Sun, Uranus, Mercury and Venus in Scorpio make it absolutely clear that there have been some financial miscalculations. Aries is said to be a robust sign and you enjoy the occasional battle, but even you could be well out of your depth now, and if matters of a legal nature are to be handled successfully you must admit to having made some mistakes. The Sun enters your angle of long-distance travel on the 23rd and if you have managed to pay your creditors and placate loved ones by this date, then you're entitled to a reprieve.

TAURUS

You can hardly expect November to be a fun or fortunate month. A series of adverse aspects to the Sun and various planets in your opposite sign of Scorpio mean that partners and loved ones will be playing up yet again and the domestic scene is more likely to contain performances of tragedy than comedy. Rehearse your lines well but don't bother to play for sympathy. Saturn in Leo throughout the whole of 1977 has probably left you downcast and bewildered, and now with Mars in the same sign there is bound to be some kind of conflict and sort-out within the family. You should, however, realize that Mars will continue to influence matters closely related to your home until well into 1978 and therefore it is up to you to try and keep the peace even when you know others are behaving outrageously.

GEMINI

The accent is on work and important career changes this month. Mars in Leo fires your imagination and makes you realize it's time to find new outlets for your creative abilities, while the Sun close to the dynamic planet Uranus in Scorpio gives you the physical energy required to up sticks. However, astrological tradition tells us that both Mars and Uranus tend to make one impulsive, impractical and inclined to rush off at a tangent. But Jupiter currently in Cancer is well placed for personal finances and a new job or promotion should add to your security. No great emotional dramas are indicated this November, even when the Sun enters your opposite sign of Sagittarius on the 23rd. It might be advisable, however, to devote a little extra time to relatives. The Mars factor is likely to make them tetchy and irritable.

CANCER

Between November 1 and 23 the Sun in Scorpio emphasizes emotional ties, love affairs and in fact anything of a very personal nature. The trouble is that Uranus – the Great Awakener of the Zodiac – is passing through the same area of your solar horoscope, and you may have some difficulty in determining exactly where your true affections lie. What you will know is that something has to be done to stabilize your financial position. Saturn in Leo throughout 1977 will certainly have drained your resources, and now that Mars has come along to complicate matters further you have no alternative but to initiate some kind of economy drive. You have, however, a considerable amount of protection from Jupiter in Cancer and all you have to do is tell relations and others it's time they picked up the tab.

LEO

If you were completely forthright and honest with relatives and associates in October, then you have nothing to fear this month. They will know that you are on a broomstick and they shouldn't argue with you. However, if – as is most probably the case – you haven't as yet said your piece, do choose your words and time carefully: there could be a confrontation you will remember with regret for months to come. With Mars in Leo now, no one can prevent you from sorting out both personal and family problems, but it is your approach and the tactics you employ which matter. The Sun, Uranus and Venus all in Scorpio are at an adverse angle to Mars and therefore loved ones and colleagues will have opinions of their own.

VIRGO

Saturn enters Virgo on November 17 and stays there until January 6, 1978. This indicates you will be in an unusually serious frame of mind and searching for solutions to very personal and intimate problems. However, try not to be too self-critical, despondent and introspective. It really is simply a question of accepting the fact that one phase or cycle in your life has come to an end and it is time to clear out all the dead wood. Mars, now in Leo, makes you hypersensitive and emotionally vulnerable, but you don't have to suffer in silence. If you think others are taking you for granted or being unnecessarily belligerent, then say so. By far the best aspects this month relate to new friendships and alliances. Jupiter in Cancer brings into your orbit people who will appreciate that you have many creative talents and abilities and who will do something constructive.

LIBRA

A great deal depends on how much you have managed to put away for the proverbial rainy day; if you are a typical Libran, it won't be much, so you will just have to work that much harder this November when the heavens open. Fortunately, with Jupiter transiting the midheaven point of your solar horoscope, career matters are going through a relatively reassuring phase and you seem to be in the unique position of being able to pick and choose. It is within the area of friendships and close relationships, however, that you have no choice other than to face the fact that one involvement at least isn't worth the tears and traumas it brings. Can you really find the courage to make the final break?

SCORPIO

The Sun now in Scorpio makes you more determined than ever to break out and do your own thing and discover in the nick of time what life is all about. You must, however, think more than twice before making any major career changes. Mars in Leo tends to make people in positions of strength or authority rather unapproachable and unco-operative. But the overall planetary picture is an encouraging one and you will eventually find the life-style and environment which suit you best. Scorpios have a bad reputation, which their true characteristics do not justify. What is certain is that those who have had the privilege of knowing you well must concede that you are the staunchest friend, ally and supporter anyone could wish for – but you won't, at any price, go against your intuition and better judgement. Nor should you.

SAGITTARIUS

Each November, until around the 23rd, while the Sun is passing through Scorpio, you start to wonder if people really do care about you or if they understand that beneath all that bravado and bonhomie you are as vulnerable and insecure as the next person. Now you are about to find out and it may mean a complete reappraisal and reassessment of relationships. However, try not to be too hard on loved ones; after all, there was a lot you didn't tell them, so how can you blame them if they were unaware of your dilemmas? Financially and materially you should have few major anxieties this month. Jupiter your ruler in Cancer makes it easier for you to raise funds and even collect what is due to you. Saturn begins a short transit of Virgo on November 17 and you start to care more about career prospects and professional prestige now.

CAPRICORN

Capricorns are seldom thought of as poets, painters or writers and yet Gray, Utrillo, Murillo, Cézanne, Chekhov and Molière were all born under your birthsign. It was Gray who wrote:

Full many a flower is born to blush unseen,

November is about relationships and their value, and perhaps you will glean a lot more about life from the words of yet another Capricorn, Sir Isaac Newton – 'I do not know what I may appear to the world, but to myself I seem to have been only a boy playing on the seashore, and diverting myself in now and then finding a smoother pebble or a prettier shell than ordinary, whilst the great ocean of truth lay all undiscovered before me.'

AQUARIUS

With Mars in your opposite sign of Leo now, you really have got your work cut out. Partnerships – whatever that word means – are likely to go through a crucial phase, but what you'll really be doing is reassessing your position after a two-year cycle during which you have been forced to accept situations which at times you may have found intolerable. Of course a great deal depends on the strength of relationships and your willingness to concede that in future the basis of all alliances will be total equality. Career matters are also highlighted in a rather spectacular way with the Sun close to your own planetary ruler. It could be the right moment to move on and find a niche for yourself higher up the ladder of success and recognition.

PISCES

Whereas most of the other signs of the Zodiac are having a tough time this month, you seem to be all set to have yourself a ball. The Sun, Uranus, Jupiter, Mercury and Venus, all in Water signs like your own, enable you to take financial or professional problems in your stride and for once enjoy emotional involvements to the full. In your solar horoscope, Scorpio represents both long-distance travel and what is termed the higher mind, and because that is where a lot of the action is now, you'll either be moving way outside your usual circle and environment or wondering why no one told you how enchanting and exhilarating life can be. There should be no borders or boundaries now. Everything is to be encompassed, experienced and enjoyed.

Monday

Hallowe'en. The Eve of the Feast of Hallowmas or All Saints.
Salmon fishing ends.
Christmas is coming closer.

Tuesday

All Saints' Day.
Sweep leaves. Check roof and gutters are leaf-free.
Fox-hunting season begins.

Wednesday

All Souls' Day. A day for remembering. The whole month is in
remembrance of all the souls in Purgatory.

Thursday

Get sparklers for Saturday. No other fireworks. Save eyes.

Friday

New Beaujolais arrives this month. Throw away old Beaujolais.

Saturday

Guy Fawkes night. Burn those leaves.
Flat racing season ends.

Sunday
6

Motherlore
Visiting spooks must be asked
'Trick or treat?' Get supplies of
sweets for treats or they will
trick you, Fiends!

Supertip
Influenza season starts. To make
a bedroom smell sweet, dissolve
a bath cube or drop some bath
oil in a jug of hot water and
leave it standing in the room.
For a sweet-smelling bed, put
talcum powder under the bottom
sheet.

Supertip
Buy a good-looking fire-
extinguisher and teach the
children how to use it.

Winter Warmer

How to Bake a Potato and What to Put in it
Method

1 Wash, scrub and dry potatoes.
2 Prick potatoes with a fork or make small slits in each with a sharp knife. If you don't, they'll burst while baking.
.3 Brush potatoes with salad oil and stand on a baking tray.
4 Bake for $1\frac{1}{2}$–2 hours (or until soft when gently pressed) on Mark 5/375°F/ 190°C.
5 Remove from oven and cut a large cross on the top of each.
6 Squeeze firmly to swell the cut, into which the filling goes.

7 Serve hot with generous pat of butter and . . .
(a) grated cheese
(b) crisp, crumbled bacon
(c) 1–2 dessertspoons sour cream sprinkled with chives
(d) scrambled eggs
(e) minced ham and cooked green peas
(f) diced sheep's kidney, fried
(g) diced mushrooms in cream
(h) chopped tomatoes with anchovy essence
(i) flaked smoked haddock and lots of butter.

Gardening

November Gardener

Keep ground clean and young plants free from voracious, plundering slugs.

Tidy up generally. Remove dead leaves from Brussels sprouts.

Traditional Dish

Cabbage and Bacon
Ingredients

1 cabbage
2 oz/50 g butter
1 peeled, crushed clove of garlic
4 rashers rindless bacon
pepper

Method

1 Remove outer leaves and stalk of cabbage, wash and shred.
2 Boil with lid firmly on saucepan for 10 minutes in half an inch of salted water, with butter, bacon and garlic. Don't overboil. Cabbage should still be crisp to chew.
3 Add plenty of pepper. Serve piping hot.

NOVEMBER

Monday
7

Supertip
Treat a black eye quickly by washing in very warm water, with a small amount of bicarbonate of soda added to it.

Tuesday
8

Wednesday
9

Supertip
If you haven't a spare wardrobe or a chest for overnight guests, use a fold-out-and-up, concertina-style, wooden clothes-dryer and provide coat hangers.

Thursday
10

Friday
11

Anniversary of end of World War I, when the Armistice was signed.

Supertip
If ivory knife handles have become yellow, rub with a cut lemon. Rinse and dry immediately.

Saturday
12

Lord Mayor of London's Procession, live or on the television.

Sunday
13

Remembrance Sunday. Red poppies are sold like those in the Flanders fields, where millions of men died in World War I.

Motherlore
'But bombs *are* unbelievable until they actually fall...'
Patrick White

Traditional Dish

Lancashire Hot-Pot
Ingredients
8 neck cutlets of lamb
3 lamb's kidneys, skinned and sliced
1 lb/450 g onions, chopped
2 lb/900 g potatoes, sliced
½ lb/225 g mushrooms, sliced or whole
½ pint/3 dl gravy (from bones) or stock
seasoning
1 teaspoon brown (HP) sauce
salt and pepper

Method
1 Arrange layers of potatoes, cutlets, onions, kidneys and mushrooms in an ovenproof casserole. Season each layer well. Put layer of potatoes on top.
2 Mix sauce with gravy or stock and pour over the dish.
3 Cook for 4 hours at Mark 1/275°F/140°C. If you like a crispy top, remove lid for last half-hour.

Reputation Maker

Pork Chops with Red Cabbage and Prunes
Ingredients
4 lean pork chops
1 lb/450 g red cabbage, washed and shredded
4 rashers streaky bacon, chopped
2 onions, chopped
3 apples, peeled, cored and chopped
16 prunes, stoned and chopped
salt and pepper
8 dessertspoons wine vinegar

Method
1 Fry chopped bacon in saucepan until crisp.
2 Add onion and sauté lightly in the bacon fat.
3 Add shredded cabbage. Cover and cook gently for 10 minutes.
4 Stir in apples, prunes, vinegar and seasonings.
5 Cook for further 10–15 minutes, stirring frequently.
6 Trim fat from chops, lightly brush with vegetable oil and put under pre-heated grill.
7 Cook briskly until golden brown on both sides, then reduce heat and continue grilling until thoroughly cooked.

NOVEMBER

Monday
14

Tuesday
15

Wednesday
16

Thursday
17

Friday
18

Saturday
19

Get materials ready for making your own Advent calendar.
(Advent starts tomorrow week.)

Sunday
20

Motherlore
Too much work never hurt
anybody. It's the anxiety that
drives you to do it that's
exhausting.

Supertip
Always invest in a spare yard of
fitted carpet for patching, a spare
roll of wallpaper and a small
spare tin of paint.

Supertip
To prevent the smell of cooking
cabbage or cauliflower, squeeze a
little lemon juice into the water.

Reputation Maker

Chicken Tangier

Ingredients

1 roasting chicken (about 4 lb/1¾–2 kg)
1 whole, unpeeled orange
juice and grated peel of 2 oranges
¼ pint/1½ dl red wine
honey
ground ginger
salt and pepper

Method

1 Clean chicken thoroughly (or remove the little plastic bag).
2 Put the orange inside the chicken.
3 Rub outside of bird with mixture of fresh orange juice, salt, pepper and ground ginger.
4 Cook in a moderate to hot oven Mark 6/400°F/200°C for 1½–2 hours until the chicken is tender.
5 Baste frequently with red wine.
6 After half an hour's cooking, brush chicken with honey. Serve garnished with grated orange peel.

Household Hint

How to Make an Advent Calendar

Ingredients

2 sheets of thin card, about 12 by 18 inches
paint *or* crayons *or* coloured pencils
newspaper to put underneath everything
an adhesive (note for mothers: Cowgum, which is what designers use, rubs off with the thumb.)
a magazine from which to cut little pictures
scissors

Method

1 Take 2 sheets of thin card. On Card A cut 25 square windows at random.
2 Put Card A on Card B and trace window positions.
3 Put Card A aside and paint or stick pretty pictures on the window spaces. *Suggestions:* a candle/a Christmas tree/ an angel/a star/Father Christmas/a sack of toys/a Christmas stocking/a Christmas cake and so on.
4 Glue underside of Card A and stick firmly to Card B. (Make sure you don't get the glue over the window spaces.)
5 Number the windows 1 to 25. Draw a Christmas Castle around the windows, then open one window a day until Christmas.

NOVEMBER

Monday
21

Start dieting for Christmas. Sweep leaves.
Book seats for Pantomime/Play/Circus (remember trains not running on Boxing Day).

Tuesday
22

Wednesday
23

Thursday
24

American Thanksgiving Day.

Friday
25

Saturday
26

Sunday
27

Advent Sunday. Christians' Countdown for Christmas.
(Advent means coming of Christ.) There are just three Sundays before Christmas.

Motherlore
Why is it easier and more virtuous for a man to be on a diet than a woman? No one groans, no one tells HIM it shows straight away on his face, that he's just fine as he is, that a girl likes something to put her arm around. No one insists he eats potatoes, even if he doesn't particularly like them; no one interferes, they only applaud. You see, a woman diets because she's vain, a man to be fit and healthy.

Motherlore
(When the Pilgrim Fathers celebrated their first successful harvest in the New World in 1621. National Holiday in U.S.A. Americans eat turkey, cranberry sauce and pumpkin pie.)

Motherlore
My favourite classified advertisement, seen in an Oxford newspaper: 'Little old lady wishes to correspond with handsome, intelligent, active young man, preferably her son.'

Traditional Dish

Margaret Costa's Christmas Pudding

Shop-bought puddings are very good indeed. If you want something better, it had better be fantastic. This is.

Ingredients

¼ lb/100 g glacé cherries
1½ lb/675 g seedless raisins
½ lb/225 g mixed candied peel
½ lb/225 g currants
¼ lb/100 g almonds
¾ lb/350 g shredded suet
¾ lb/350 g fine breadcrumbs

8 eggs
6 tablespoons brandy, rum or whisky
¼ pint/1½ dl brown ale or stout
1 small teaspoon cinnamon ⎫
1 small teaspoon nutmeg ⎬ optional
good pinch coriander or ⎭
  allspice

Method

1 The quantities given will fill one 2-pint and one 1½-pint pudding basin. Basins should be well-buttered and the bottoms lined with a round of buttered greaseproof paper.

2 Cut the glacé cherries into halves or quarters; if the raisins are large, halve them too.

3 Flour the dried fruit lightly and rub with fingers as though making pastry. Then put into a sieve and shake well.

4 Pour boiling water over almonds to blanch. Remove skin then chop or slice them.

5 Mix all fruit and nuts well with the breadcrumbs and shredded suet. If wanted, add cinnamon, nutmeg, coriander or allspice.

6 Beat eggs hard until light and frothy and stir into the dry ingredients.

7 Stir in the brandy and beer, enough to make a mixture which drops easily from the spoon, but not too runny.

8 Divide mixture into pudding basins, filling them about three-quarters full. Smooth over the tops, making a very slight hollow in the middle.

9 Cut out double rounds of greaseproof paper and butter well on one side. Cover puddings with paper rounds, buttered side down, and tie on a scalded, well wrung out, lightly floured cloth.

10 Stand basins on a rack in a large saucepan or fish kettle and pour on boiling water to come two-thirds of the way up the sides of the basins.

11 Cover pan and steam for at least 2 hours, topping up with more *boiling* water if necessary. A 1½-pint pudding needs 6 hours altogether and a 2-pint pudding 7–8 hours. Keep in a dark, dry, cool and airy cupboard until wanted.

December

ARIES

So, Aries the Ram, you have probably butted and battered your way through yet another year; now it is time to ask, what did it get you? Are you happier, more relaxed and at peace with yourself? Vincent van Gogh – like you, born under Aries – said: 'To express hope by some star, the eagerness of a soul by a sunset radiance. Certainly there is nothing in that of stereoscopic realism but is it not something that actually exists?' The year ends as it began with Pluto in direct opposition to your natal Sun and you must continue to strive for the right common denominator in partnerships and close relationships because if you don't, you will be plagued by home and domestic difficulties in 1978. Careerwise, the outlook is a decidedly encouraging one but at some point or other, you are going to have to return home.

TAURUS

Financial obligations and commitments are your main concerns this month; no matter how practical and persevering you have been in the year that is past, you are still hard-pressed to pay your way. But Taurians are not defeatists and somehow you will manage to scrape through. Don't, however, believe that emotional difficulties can be resolved by just biding your time – they can't. You have to allow others their freedom if you want them to stay. Maybe it is you who wants to be freed and discover contentment and security elsewhere, but with Uranus in your opposite sign of Scorpio adversely aspected by Mars in Leo you are in a way shackled by the vows and promises you have made. Not until late 1978 can you hope to divest yourself of present responsibilities.

GEMINI

With the Sun, Neptune, Venus and Mercury all in your opposite sign of Sagittarius this December, there are bound to be moments when partnerships become a problem. Neptune is a nebulous planet and you may be driven to distraction because loved ones are vague, unco-operative and unwilling to be reasonable. You find it almost impossible to cope with what you consider to be unnecessary emotional dramas and this is perhaps why you feel so out in the cold. Others cannot communicate and presume you don't really care. If you learnt anything at all in 1977, it should have been that a problem shared is a problem halved: it really does not matter whether you are worried about your job, money or emotional security, you must be prepared to take others into your confidence.

CANCER

As all the major planetary movements are now in the lower half of your solar horoscope, it is safe to assume your major problems will be ones of a fairly mundane nature and will relate to everyday life rather than ambitions or aspirations. However, Jupiter remains in your own birthsign until the end of the year and after spending a period in retrograde motion returns in April 1978 for another 6 months' stay. So nothing should really get you down, although of course there will be times when you do not feel you have the energy to battle on. The best thing you can do is compare your position to what it was a year ago and perhaps you will admit that on balance you're better off.

LEO

Were it not for the fact that Mars is in retrograde motion to your own birthsign this month, you would be having a lovely time; but an afflicted Mars means you become too restless and impatient and can't understand why others won't commit themselves or co-operate. You would save yourself a whole heap of trouble if you just sat back, pondered awhile and let loved ones take the initiative for a change. If you do insist on answers and explanations, it could be a very dreary and depressing month at home. Saturn in the first degree of Virgo throughout the whole of December means your financial position could be undermined by developments and circumstances way beyond your control.

VIRGO

Virgos are not very good at taking things on trust – you have to know how and you have to be sure. December is one month when you just can't demand answers and explanations because after the 12th, when your own ruling planet Mercury will be in retrograde motion, what you are told will be far from the complete truth. Saturn in the first degree of Virgo is giving you a foretaste of what you can expect in 1978 and just how many areas of your life are going to change. Don't jump to conclusions and imagine it is all going to be disastrous, because it's not. Ask any Leo at the moment whether or not their experiences over the last year or so have not in fact given them a greater breadth of vision and made them realize, as you surely will, that if you can take the knocks and discard what is outworn and out of date, you emerge stronger and more resolute than ever.

LIBRA

One – not often sung – song of Noel Coward's begins, 'Sweet day remain for men, clear in my memory; when my heart's chilled by the snows of December – let me remember, let me remember'. As the year draws to a close you will have a lot you want to recall but perhaps more you would prefer to forget. Nevertheless, don't give way to despondency and negative thinking this month, even though you may feel disenchanted by relationships and can't imagine why others only want you as a best friend. Tell them you have enough best friends now to last you a lifetime and that you need something more meaningful. Exactly what is a meaningful relationship anyway? One where you will be wanted, admired and sought after is at work, although it may take a complete change of job to get the financial security you want.

SCORPIO

It would be lovely to predict that December was going to be a fantastic month for you, but with Uranus in Scorpio adversely aspected by Mars the portents seem to indicate that it is in fact going to be the reverse. You will have to fight every inch of the way and will still find it difficult to discover permanent solutions to either personal or professional problems. Mars in particular, which is in retrograde motion after the 13th, stirs up trouble at work, and those who have the power to promote or deflate you will have to be charmed out of existence. Only one important planetary aspect continues to give you hope, Jupiter in Cancer – but it will only be by travelling far from your home that you will be able to reap its benefit.

SAGITTARIUS

With four planets – Saturn and Jupiter, Mars and Mercury – all in retrograde motion this month, you can only expect to be confused mentally and emotionally. Saturn in Virgo makes you wonder if it isn't the right time to make important career changes – it isn't. Jupiter in Cancer indicates partnership finances and business affairs are not what you had imagined while Mars in Leo disrupts travel plans and arrangements. But it is Mercury in your own birthsign which really bedevils all your attempts to make relationships work. Not, then, a very exciting or encouraging end to the year. No Sagittarian likes to be left in the dark or without direction. However, at this time you would be well advised to leave your options open and not become flustered if you can't quite tie up all the loose ends.

CAPRICORN

Not until the Sun enters your own birthsign on December 22 will you feel sufficiently confident and energetic to make any drastic changes in either your personal or professional life. This is one of those months when you just cannot gauge with any degree of accuracy how others will react or place your complete faith in offers of assistance. Mars in Leo means partnership finances are at a low ebb, and if you yourself are not in trouble, then it will be others who have to be bailed out. Jupiter in your opposite sign of Cancer also means that in spite of all your hard work and determination your progress seems to be temporarily blocked. Capricorns are born patient – well, at least you don't believe in dissipating your time and energies in wishful thinking.

AQUARIUS

If only Mars would shift itself, then there would be a lot fewer disgruntled and disenchanted Aquarians about. But Mars will remain in your opposite sign of Leo throughout the whole of December and the first three weeks of January 1978; therefore it would be foolish to imagine that partners and loved ones are suddenly going to change their ways or alter their tactics and let you off the hook. So, try to memorize these words of Montaigne: 'A good marriage, if there is such a thing, rejects the company and conditions of love. It tries to imitate those of friendship.' A sobering thought. Joint financial arrangements are probably part of the overall problem at the moment, and now that Saturn has moved into Virgo for a while you are not likely to find long-term solutions just yet. On no account should you enter into litigation.

PISCES

You should have enjoyed a lot of 1977, and although you have to do some serious thinking about your career prospects this December the outlook remains an encouraging one. Jupiter in Cancer and Uranus in Scorpio continue to convince you that your attitude and approach are the right ones and that you don't have to change or adapt just because others are more pushy and more self-assertive. You are now in one of the most creative and productive phases of your life and if you feel that your talents would be better employed elsewhere, move on. What you can't do is disentangle yourself from partnerships and love affairs. Saturn will soon begin its transit of Virgo, your opposite sign of the Zodiac, and when Saturn says 'Stay!' there is no escape.

Monday
28

Christmas is *really* coming. You'll have to do something now.

Tuesday
29

Wednesday
30

St Andrew's Day. Feast of patron saint of Scotland.
Have a Scotch.

Thursday
1

Friday
2

Saturday
3

Sunday
4

Festival of Chanukah, also known as the Feast of Lights,

Supertip
Always deal with a stain on cloth as quickly as possible and *never* with hot water, because that sets the stain and you'll never get it out.

Supertip
Don't waste today.

Motherlore
The Festival of Chanukah, begins tonight in synagogues and Jewish homes where they light the first candle in the Menorah, the eight-branch Chanukah candelabra. One more candle will be lit every night of the eight-day festival until the whole Menorah is lit up. The festival commemorates the successful revolt more than 2000 years ago of the Hasmoneans led by Judas Maccabeus against the Syrian oppressors in Palestine.

Household Hint

Time to plan your CHRISTMAS COUNTDOWN.

Cards: List/buy/write/send.

Presents: List/buy/wrap/send. Don't forget extra anonymous presents (thin black cigars for males, deliciously scented soap for females, or vice versa).

Decorations: Check last year's decorations to see what's broken, bent, or frayed. Decide on schemes for front door/fireplace/table/rest of the house.

Tree: Check last year's decorations. Straighten out fairy's wings, etc. Buy new decorations and lights.

Buy tree and stand on cloth or rug to avoid pine needles everywhere.

Decorate tree.

Drink: Plan and order now.

Food: Plan and order now, except for extra bread and milk. There's a note to remind you about that on December 22. Order Christmas turkey, goose or other chosen joint. Extra supplies.

Pudding: Make, order or buy. If making, long slow steaming will darken a pudding as much as age.

Cake: ditto. Don't make cake and pudding on the same day because it's too exhausting. Cook double quantities of both, so you'll have a vintage pudding and cake in '78. Don't marzipan and ice next year's cake now. Dedicated bakers who've already made their cake will want to decorate it; make almond and royal icing/mince pies/tarts. Store them in airtight containers or freeze.

Plan party food for New Year's Eve and Hogmanay celebrations. Phew!

Gardening

December Gardener
Back to the fire.

Winter Warmer

Yankee Corned Beef Hash

Ingredients
1 large onion, peeled and sliced
1½ lb/675 g corned beef, diced
1½ lb/675 g potatoes, boiled and diced
4 oz/100 g dripping or fat
¼ pint/1½ dl milk
salt and pepper

Method
1 Fry onion in hot fat until transparent.
2 Mix meat, potatoes, seasoning, milk and add to onions in pan.
3 When well mixed, flatten to fit pan.
4 Cook over moderate heat until brown underneath.
5 Toast top side under grill until crisp and golden brown.

DECEMBER

Monday
5

Tuesday
6

Oxford *v* Cambridge rugby match at Twickenham.

Wednesday
7

Supertip
Use rubber gloves, or a damp sponge of foam rubber, to pick up cotton, etc. from carpets or upholstery.

Thursday
8

Friday
9

Saturday
10

Grouse and Black Game shooting ends.

Sunday
11

Plan for New Year sales. Put aside money before it's all spent on Christmas.

Supertip
Use paper clips for Christmas tree decorations; they are easier to suspend things with than cotton.

Reputation Maker

Quick Curry Party:
Lamb Curry/Prawn Curry/Egg Curry and Egg Mayonnaise

(Serves 10; double the quantities for 20)

Ingredients

2½ lb/generous kg good boneless stewing lamb

½ lb/225 g dried prawns (fresh or frozen)

10 hardboiled eggs

5 large onions, chopped

3 cloves garlic, crushed

3 rounded dessertspoons curry powder

1½ dessertspoons tomato concentrate

2 oz/50 g butter

4 crushed cardamom seeds

½ pint/3 dl stock (or chicken bouillon cube)

2 pinches ginger

½ tablespoon double cream

1 cleaned lettuce

¼ pint/1½ dl mayonnaise

Method

1 Cut lamb into small cubes.

2 In a large saucepan, melt butter, add onions and garlic; cook for 5 minutes over medium heat. Do not allow to brown.

3 Add 2 rounded dessertspoons of curry powder and cook, stirring for 5 minutes over a low heat. Add tomato paste and cardamom seeds.

4 Now divide the curry sauce equally into 3 saucepans.

5 Add 1 dessertspoon curry powder to the first saucepan, then add the lamb. Mix well, cover pan and simmer until meat is tender (about 40 minutes).

6 Add 2 pinches ginger to the second saucepan, add the prawns and mix well. Cover pan and simmer: 10 minutes for dried prawns, 5 minutes for fresh or frozen.

7 Cut 5 eggs in half and heat gently in the third curry, to which the double cream has been added.

8 Halve remaining hardboiled eggs and serve cold on a bed of lettuce with mayonnaise on a separate dish. This is for people who don't like curry.

9 Label to egg curry HOT, the prawn curry HOTTER and the lamb curry HOTTEST.

10 Serve with fluffy boiled rice and side dishes of pickled cabbage, onions, coconut, bananas, gherkins, cucumbers and hot poppadoms, heated in a low oven.

DECEMBER

Monday
12

Office party season starts. Practise reproachful smile.

Tuesday
13

Wednesday
14

Buy new Superwoman diary.

Thursday
15

Friday
16

Supertip
There are some things that a girl can never get enough of, such as love, money and teatowels. They make a useful spare present for females and enliven Christmas washing-up.

Saturday
17

Sunday
18

Supertip
Why not end the constant mess in the medicine cupboard by throwing out almost everything except the motorist's first-aid kit? Once they have done their job, medicines should be thrown away, because what is good for one illness might be bad for another.

Reputation Maker

Party Dips:

Shirley MacLaine's Avocado Dip

Ingredients

4 ripe avocado pears
2–3 cloves garlic, crushed
2 peeled tomatoes, sieved
1 medium onion, finely chopped
2 teaspoons lemon juice
1 teaspoon vinegar
chopped chives and paprika
1 tablespoon oil
salt and pepper

Method

1 Halve the avocado pears, remove stones and scoop out flesh into a large bowl.
2 With wooden spoon mix in garlic.
3 Add tomatoes, then onion, then everything else.
4 Season and sharpen to taste with lemon juice.
5 Beat to a paste, then pat down in bowl. Sprinkle with chopped chives and paprika.
6 Alternatively, spread on pieces of hot, dry toast.

Basic Cream Cheese Dip

Ingredients

$\frac{1}{4}$ pint/$1\frac{1}{2}$ dl cream cheese
$\frac{1}{4}$ pint/$1\frac{1}{2}$ dl cream
juice of one lemon
2 big grated onions
salt and pepper

Method

1 Thin the cream cheese to a suitable consistency with the cream.
2 Mix in all other ingredients to taste. Chill and serve.
3 *For variations* add a few dashes Worcester sauce *or* chopped anchovies *or* red and green pepper.

Asparagus and Prawn Dip

Ingredients

4 tablespoons canned asparagus, chopped
2–3 oz/50–75 g peeled prawns, very finely chopped
2 cartons natural yoghurt (10-oz/275-g size)
salt and pepper
green olives to garnish

Method

Mix all ingredients together in a bowl and dot with olives.

DECEMBER

Monday
19

Tuesday
20

Wednesday
21

It's officially winter.

Thursday
22

Remember to buy or order extra milk and bread supplies for Christmas.

Friday
23

Saturday
24

Sunday
25

Christ's birthday. Quarter Day.

Motherlore
Experience helps, but not very much.

Motherlore
It's the winter solstice, when the sun enters the sign of Capricornus. The sun is at its most southerly point in relation to the equator. Shortest day of the year. Longest night. Enjoy yourself.

Supertip
How about rereading some good books over Christmas? Not Proust, but Household Appliance instructions? As well as making sure you're getting the most out of them you might even be inspired to use the bits you have forgotten about, such as the paint spray attachment to the vacuum cleaner.

Traditional Dish

Cumberland Sauce

Ingredients

- 2 large tablespoons redcurrant jelly (Tiptree's is best if you don't make your own)
- 2 tablespoons port
- 1 small orange
- 1 small lemon
- 1 level teaspoon dried mustard powder
- 1 level teaspoon ground ginger

Can be made well in advance and stored in a screw-top jar in the bottom of the refrigerator

Method

1 Using a sharp knife pare rind from orange and lemon. Cut into very thin, small strips.

2 Boil rind in water for 5 minutes, then drain well to remove any bitterness.

3 Put port and redcurrant jelly in pan, melt over low heat for 5–10 minutes until jelly melts.

4 Mix ginger and mustard together in bowl. Add juice of half a lemon. Stir until smooth.

5 Add juice of whole orange, then the redcurrant jelly mixture, then the orange and lemon strips. Mix thoroughly.

6 Delicious cold with hot or cold ham, tongue, duck and game. Also good warmed up.

Reputation Maker

Christmas Cider Cup

Ingredients

- ¼ bottle ordinary brandy
- 1 quart/generous litre medium cider
- 1 syphon soda water
- 2 lemons
- 10 very thin slices cucumber
- 4 rounded tablespoons granulated sugar
- 1 thin-skinned sweet orange, sliced very thinly

Method

1 Thinly peel the rind from 2 lemons, squeeze and strain the juice.

2 Put all ingredients into a large jug and chill. Just before serving, remove lemon peel and cucumber slices and turn into a punch bowl. Squirt on 1 syphon soda water.

DECEMBER

Monday

Boxing Day. Bank Holiday. 364 shopping days to Christmas. Pantomime season starts. But still no trains to get there.

Tuesday

Another Bank Holiday (except in Scotland).

Wednesday
28

First sales start. During this year it will have rained *somewhere* in Britain on approximately 360 days. Look for cheap electric clothes-dryer in sales. More sales next month.

Thursday
29

Friday
30

Buy extra drink for New Year's Eve tomorrow.

Saturday
31

Happy Hogmanay.

Sunday

Supertip

Keep a special box for old newspapers. Only when it is full will it be emptied; then the Liberal Party can have it if they want. Meanwhile, if anybody wants to look up back numbers, clean his shoes or light a fire, he will know where he can go.

Supertip

Strip any remaining turkey carcass and make meat into fricassees, pâtés or pasties. If possible, freeze and produce later when Christmas is forgotten.

Poor Girl's Cheese Spread
(good for stale Stilton)
Grate leftover bits of stale cheese. Boil a little milk in a saucepan (about 2 tablespoons to 1 oz/ 25 g cheese) with a knob of butter. Pepper well; add cheese and melt. Pour into cheese pot and wait to set, whereupon you will have Cheese Spread.

Cheese (or Smoked Haddock) Soufflé

Ingredients

3 tablespoons flour
3 tablespoons butter
1 cup cream or milk
1 cup grated cheese (or smoked haddock)

3 egg yolks
4 egg whites
salt and pepper

Method

1 Make a thick creamy sauce using the butter, flour and milk.
2 When thick and boiling, add cheese (or smoked haddock), season to taste.
3 Beat egg yolks, add a little of the hot sauce, stir and return to pan with the rest of the sauce.
4 Cook for a few minutes, stirring all the time, and do not let the mixture boil. Cool mixture to room temperature.
5 Beat egg whites until stiff and peaky, fold into cooled mixture.

6 Pour mixture into ungreased 7-inch (17-cm) soufflé dish; tie a collar of greaseproof paper around the dish, rising about 2 inches above it, to prevent the soufflé from flopping over the sides.
7 For a really professional effect gently score the top of the soufflé with a thin knife, making a circle shape in the centre.
8 Bake for 1 hour at the top of the oven Mark 4/350°F/180°C, until top is browned and firm. Make sure everyone is sitting at the table and serve at once.

When making soufflés, always remember . . .

a Have the soufflé dish prepared before starting.
b The thick sauce which forms the basis of the soufflé must be thick and slightly cooled before adding the egg whites.

c Make sure you have the right oven temperature.
d Serve immediately it is cooked, otherwise it will flop. Time from the cooking when it's to be served.

Household Hint

Lentil Soup

Amazing discovery . . . you don't *have* to soak lentils overnight. Just boil a cupful of lentils in 1½ pints (scant litre) chicken stock (homemade or use a Knorr Chicken bouillon cube). Throw in a ham bone and/or bacon rind and simmer for ¾ hour or until lentils are cooked. Do NOT let the lentils become too soft - they are meant to be crunchy.

NOTES FOR 1978